KAREN MILLER

MY LIFE AS A SISTER WIFE

What you don't know *can* hurt you.

DAY agency publishing

Day Agency Publishing
South Jordan, UT 84009

Print and e-Book Interior Design: Dayna Linton, Day Agency Publishing
Cover Design: Jeffery Olsen
Photo credit: LeAnne Miller

Library of Congress Control Number: Pending

ISBN: 978-0-9998597-5-9 (Paperback)
ISBN: 978-0-9998597-8-0 (e-Book)

First Edition: 2018

10 9 8 7 6 5 4 3 2 1

Printed in the USA

AUTHOR'S NOTE

Some terms used in my story which will help you understand a little better.

The Order: The religiously based, financially and socially committed, loosely organized number of individuals such as ours.

The Principle: A common name for living plural marriage.

The Property: The parcel of land in the Cedar Valley that Frank was to develop.

For my family, who are my why.

MY LIFE AS A SISTER WIFE

What you don't know *can* hurt you.

PROLOGUE

———◦✦◦———

OFTEN, WHILE AT THE bottom of a dumpster scavenging for food, the thought that I could write a book about this most unusual ritual would enter my mind. Mostly, it was just something you say without any real intention attached to it. Nonetheless, the first tentative steps had begun.

Not until I had left plural marriage, did I give the thought any serious attention. Only after friends and co-workers began to suggest that my story needed to be told did I seriously begin to think about it. Would anyone really want to know about this secret life?

My mind would race through years of memories with their enduring emotions. At first, I would write down random thoughts on scraps of paper and put them in a shoe box, which seemed to be a good place at the time, to await some kind of commitment on my part down the road.

At one time I thought that my journals would be good

source material for an inspirational book. All the wives in our family were expected to keep a daily journal. At first, back then, I would write my feelings and perceptions of my experience and interaction with family members. That quickly changed when my then-husband Frank asked for my journal to read.

The problem was that I had written some very personal and vulnerable things. Worse yet, though Frank did not use my name, he betrayed my feelings in front of other people by using them as an object lesson on how a wife ought to think and behave. After that, I wrote only the most ordinary and mundane things with little hint of emotion. The outline of events is there, with some feelings, but not much of a personal nature. However, the emotions came roaring back with startling intensity once I began this memoir.

With the encouragement and assistance of family and friends, this project grew as did my confidence that there was enough material for a book, even if it was small, and that it was good stuff. With no experience in writing, I set about to write and rewrite again. Some thoughts were keepers, some were tossed, some things I felt best left buried in the past. When I felt in need of direction, I would ask friends, "What kinds of things would you find interesting in a book such as mine?" The answer was always, "How did it make you feel?"

Some may see this as an exposé on polygamy, but quite the contrary, it is simply the telling of how it was for me and how I came to move from its shadow to the fulfilling life I now lead.

It is my hope that this book will reach a broad spectrum of society, delivering the assurance that there is no good reason for anyone to be treated in a demeaning or dehumanizing manner. Everyone should have the reasonable expectation of being treated with dignity and kindness.

When an individual is able to see that they are not being treated properly, and if they can find the inner strength to seek other alternatives, they will thrive. Go, stay, or fight for change. The choice is yours. It will be an arduous journey and a little painful, often slowed by second guessing ourselves and our motives, but well worth the growing pains.

BY WAY OF EXPLANATION

———◦◆◦———

THIS BOOK IS NOT a novel. It is however, a collage
of memories, snippets if you will, of my life as
a plural wife. A glimpse into everyday life, along
with some of the extraordinary lengths our husband went
to so as to obtain and keep control of his family. My book
can only present fragments of an entire culture, as well
as a lifetime. It has to be experienced or at least closely
observed to get the full effect. Time and possibly wisdom
will not allow for that.

The events are not sequential but are grouped in cat-
egories such as the homes we lived in, how we were expected to conduct family life. All of this is woven with a
common thread that will present an intimate view of our
lives. I have often thought; how did an independent young
woman wind up in a mess like this?

Insights into my early life are to show a contrast of
my fairly normal childhood for that time to the type of

childhood my children experienced. They allow me to show some cultural differences as well. As I have thought about it, my fear of my dad may have contributed to my willingness to live under a controlled, male-dominated structure. Apparently, even a strong, independent woman can fall under psychological manipulation when it feels familiar. Even though it may pinch you, putting on a comfortable old shoe is easy to do.

I also think that when I was presented with an opportunity to live plural marriage, I felt special. I was going to be one of the few who was willing to live every law that God had established, even though the mainstream LDS church was no longer practicing it. In 1890, it was revealed by the Lord to President Wilford Woodruff that the church was no longer to continue living that law.

1

LET'S START AT THE BEGINNING ...
A VERY GOOD PLACE TO START

Our story begins in one hemisphere and plays
out in another.

In 1944, many things were going on in the
world. The Second World War continued to rage throughout Europe and in the Pacific with evil unleashing its fury
on mankind. 1944 saw President Roosevelt elected to an
unprecedented fourth term in America. Fifteen-year-old
Anne Frank was captured and sent to a concentration
camp, leaving her diary, a testament to her courage. This
same year, a kidney dialysis machine was invented by Wil-
lem Kopf, and Benjamin Green invented a substance to
protect our soldiers from sunburn and went on to create
the Coppertone Company. In munitions factories across

the country, thousands of women, personified by "Rosie the Riveter" worked tirelessly to support our men in the war effort.

There is a saying that a baby is God's way of showing mankind that life should go on. On a hot February day, I made my debut in life.

Crown Street Women's Hospital in Sydney, Australia was typical of the day: long open wards, lined with crisply made beds, a tri-fold screen to provide privacy for patients, metal wash basins and bedpans that would be sterilized in autoclaves. The nursing staff was made up of nursing students who worked in the hospital for their tuition while also attending classes. The registered nurses were known as nursing sisters, perhaps in reference to a time when hospitals had a religious connection. All wore well-starched bib aprons, with the appropriate caps to delineate their stations.

Labor and delivery was in the same type of open ward behind a tri-fold screen where women experienced the pains of labor, just as their mothers and grandmothers had before them. It was in such a setting that I came screaming into the world—a great set of lungs and so much thick dark hair that the nurses named me "Minnie ha, ha," after the wife of legendary Hiawatha.

For the first few years of my life, we lived with my mom's parents in their small home. Being the first grandchild, I was thoroughly spoiled and was the apple of my grandpa's eye. The story goes that grandpa would come home from work, bellow "Where's my boompsie," pick me up even if I was asleep, play with me, then put me back in the crib and I would go right back to sleep. Growing up,

Grandma would say that she could hang me out on the clothes line and I would sleep right through it.

There is drama in every family; ours was no different. Grandma didn't like Dad because she wanted Mom to marry someone else. So, things were tense at home, I was told.

A few years after I was born, we moved into a detached room which was called a "sleep out," a few steps from Dad's parent's back door. As I grew older, I could see there were stark differences in the quality of life of each of my grandparents.

Mom's parents, the Tideswell's, lived in an older suburb which had utilities, including a flushing outhouse. It had a water tank up high and you had to pull a chain to release the water. My dad's family, the Smiths, lived in the outskirts of the suburbs and did not enjoy such luxuries. Nana had an enormous wood-burning cook stove which she managed with great finesse, including baking bread and pies. But the kitchen became unimaginably hot in the summer.

Mom cooked our meals in that kitchen and we spent much of our time outdoors or in our tiny room, which only had space for our beds and dressers. There was an outhouse that I had to make a run for, even in the middle of the night as I was afraid of the dark. There was another detached room where we bathed, which had a tub, shower and cold running water. Hot water came from an old copper wash tub that was kept and heated in yet another shed. We hauled buckets of water and emptied them into the bathtub.

I was about seven years old when my parents were able to get a government loan to build their own home. This is where I lived until I left home at twenty-one years of age. Not many homes were built from brick as it was very expensive. Our house was made from a substance called Fibro, made of compressed synthetic fibers much like particle board. Fibro is a brand name of a popular building material and is still in use in Australia. With wet weather, the substance would become very damp and Mom had to watch for mold.

I became a latchkey kid, with both parents working and dad holding down a second job to pay off the mortgage. I learned my work ethic from my parents and am grateful to them.

I come from a long line of beer drinkers. There were many summer Sunday afternoons spent at the Tideswell's with Mom's siblings and their families. The adults would be sitting outside in the warm weather, enjoying glasses of cold beer and each other's company. The cousins, including myself, thought we were very clever as we drained the last few drops from the tall brown bottles the adults had discarded, thinking no one noticed.

Christmas came with humid, ninety plus degree weather. We had spindly Norfolk pine trees sitting in a bucket of water while hoping that the needles didn't dry out and fall off, decorated with baubles, tinsel and "Santa Snow." We had never seen snow, but Christmas cards had pictures of it even though we lived in the subtropics.

Mom's family would gather for Christmas dinner. There was always a hot meal, which was never complete without the traditional Christmas pudding into which was placed three penny and six penny pieces and a one shilling piece, all of which was for good luck in the year to come. These puddings were prepared weeks in advance, hung to cure, reheated and served with whipped cream or English custard. Children were careful not to swallow any money, licking pudding from each deliciously sticky coin.

Notwithstanding these happy memories, my childhood was overshadowed by a deep fear of my dad. There were few tender moments spent with him.

Dad made it clear on numerous occasions that his ideal was only he and mom, just the two of them. I think my birth was an accident. Perhaps his own hard life as a child brought him to his brutal style of parenting. Corporal punishment was the way of the day—spare the rod, spoil the child! He frequently used his belt or a stick on my butt or a smack across my face, often leaving a bloody nose or ringing ears to "teach me a lesson."

I would make the most transparent excuses for marks on my face. A neighbor asked how the red mark came to be, I told her that it was sunburn. The welt showed a reverse image of my father's hand, however. I was not the most obedient child, as I would often play where I wasn't supposed to because all my friends did it, which included playing in a swamp that had snakes. I often went home covered in slimy algae.

Parenting was different in those days. Children were punished as opposed to being taught. I was so afraid of Dad that I would tell the most transparent lie in the hopes of not being punished, but I would get it worse for doing so.

Nonetheless, as I have analyzed the situation, it's a hard thing for a child to be so afraid of a parent. I would feel nauseated at the thought of being alone with him. Heart pounding, hands trembling, occasionally wetting myself at the prospect of being punished by him when I finished walking home from school.

Such was most of my childhood, leaving me with the resolve to never beat my children. School summer vacation spent at Grandma and Grandpa Tideswell's home (where I was never beaten or punished) was a relief and refuge for me; so passed the years of elementary school.

High school was an adventure of a different sort, compared with how things are now.

Australia was very British at the time in that there were boy's high schools and girl's high schools. There were also parochial schools, but this was the public-school system. Part of the excitement of starting high school was that we wore uniforms.

The girls wore a belted tunic, navy in color, with three wide pleats front and back, made of cotton for the summer time and wool in the winter. We also had black stockings held up with a garter belt and polished black lace-up shoes. We wore a long sleeved white shirt (sleeves were never to be rolled up) with a tie of the school colors, a navy blazer with the school insignia on the top pocket, a hat with a band of the school colors and finally, navy gloves.

All of this was very exciting at first, sort of a rite of passage. We were expected to be in full uniform to and from school. Being out of uniform to any degree, if caught, was punishable with detention. Of course, the novelty of the uniform soon wore off. Then, as soon as I was off the bus, I would be down to my tunic and blouse before I was halfway down the street.

After I graduated from high school, I was employed as a receptionist for a law firm in downtown Sydney. This gave me my first sense of autonomy, along with earning my own money. I began to feel, for the first time, a sense of self-worth. I loved the bustle of the city, all the people and stores. Almost everyone used public transportation in those days and I didn't mind the long, crowded train rides to and from work.

Dad drove buses for the city, often double-deckers, which was a bragging point for me as a child. He also held down another job at night to pay off the mortgage once he realized how much interest he would be paying. During this time, Mom worked five-and-a-half days a week for a paint manufacturing company called Taubman's Paint, which is still in business today. This didn't leave her much time for anything else. I would go grocery shopping for her most Saturday mornings to help.

The nearest shopping center was a fifteen-minute bus ride to a suburb named Kogarah, which happened to be where the train station was. In those days, there were no supermarkets. There would be a butcher shop, a dry goods shop with flour and sugar and so on, a green grocer for produce, a newspaper shop for newspapers, magazines, paperback books and the like. There was no home delivery except for milk. We would leave out a metal container on the doorstep, along with money, and the milk man would ladle out the amount paid for.

There was also a chemist shop for dispensing prescriptions and a clothing store. I'm sure there were others, but I don't remember them all. Close to the bus stop, there was a small restaurant where milkshakes were sold. They were made of milk, flavoring and a minute scoop of vanilla ice cream which was stirred in a metal blending machine, just like in the old movies.

2

THE WINDS OF CHANGE
BEGIN TO STIR

MOST PEOPLE IN THOSE days dressed very casually, especially on a weekend. One Saturday morning while shopping, I saw two young men dressed in dark suits, a white shirt and tie, a style that caused them to stand out among the busy flow of people. No one wore suits unless they were businessmen or going to a wedding or a funeral. They were approaching people at random and speaking to them. I thought it was curious, not only their dress, but their actions. The next week, they were at it again. This was unusual; you normally would never see this type of thing. I wondered what they were up to.

A third week came, and they were there again, but they didn't stop me. *That's it!* I thought, so I stopped one of them to ask what they were doing. He looked so happy to talk to me and began to shake my hand in the most enthusiastic manner. They were missionaries for the Church of Jesus Christ of Latter-day Saints (nicknamed the Mormons) and were asking people if they had heard of the church and if they would like to know more. They were also Americans.

My mom had a Mormon friend whom I had met a few years before. All I knew about her was that she drank milk, nothing else. The missionaries invited me to a barbeque that evening, which turned out to be an opportunity for them to talk about their church.

What a rip off, I thought, *this is not a social gathering.* But respected the gumption it took to stop people cold in the street. I found myself interested in what they had to say and decided to meet with them at a member's home the following week.

(I must mention here that my dad, as with many of his generation, did not have fond feelings toward Americans in general following the Second World War. According to my parents, American service men would chant things such as, "We won the war," in the streets of Sydney. All the allies fought fiercely, but I guess that type of thing rubbed Dad and others like him the wrong way. This made it difficult to be open about meeting with the Mormons, as he thought of it as an American church.)

Neither of my parents were religious, but I had been attending a church a few blocks from home so my interest in religion was not a surprise to them. But when they discovered my interest in the Mormons, you would have thought I wanted to join the Communist party or shave my head! I was eighteen, almost nineteen, but I had to wait until I turned nineteen to be baptized. My parents said that I also had to read the entire *Book of Mormon* before doing so.

I was not much of a reader back then, not that my mom didn't try. She was an avid reader. So, I read the introduction and every word of the chapter headings. I felt justified in this bit of trickery, as the entire book would have taken me months to read! The *Book of Mormon* is scripture to the Mormons, along with the Bible, but by this time I knew in my heart and in my mind that this was what I had been looking for as my path to follow God.

Predictably, my parents did not attend my baptism and the very thing which was filling my soul became a wedge between me and my parents. I did, however, receive a stiff warning not to try and influence any of my cousins toward "my" church. How do you not want to share something you find so fulfilling, that opens your mind to things you have wondered about but couldn't figure out? I respected their wishes at the time, though I regret it now.

On Sunday mornings, I would walk miles to the train station to get to church, staying there almost all day and then returning by the same route. My dad was very critical of this and would laugh at my "foolishness," but I didn't care. Hostility increased at home, not so much from Mom, but Dad was vehement in his distaste toward and criticism of my new-found religion.

There were other young women at the church I attended who were in similar circumstances, feeling the pressure at home because of our religious choices. At first, we considered moving into an apartment together, but I thought that would only worsen already hard feelings. Not only that, "good girls" in those days lived at home until they were married.

A year or so later, those girls and I decided to travel together, which was a socially acceptable way to see something of the world and broaden our horizons. We were all hoping that time would soothe wounds in our families. I had worked a second job to earn money for my passage and had little left to tide me over once we got to Calgary, Alberta in Canada until I could get a job. That seemed of little consequence, as I was young and able to work, which left me feeling invincible, as most young people do.

3

OUR JOURNEY BEGINS

THE YEAR WAS 1965. It was a cold July day with a strong southerly wind blowing. As the tug boats strained to pull our ship from the wharf, we could feel the deck shudder beneath our feet. Family and friends stood on the wharf bundled against a bitter wind to bid us farewell. A combination of excitement and adrenaline filled me, along with a sadness that my sweet mom was so sad. Once under our own steam, we moved into the main shipping channel of Sydney Harbor, slipping beneath the Sydney Harbor bridge. We were awed by the enormity of its great single span.

Kerry, Pauline, Lynette and I attended the Hurstville ward, one of several Mormon meeting houses in the Sydney area. We had become friends over the two years we knew each other. From our vantage point, we could see the many green and yellow ferry boats that we had each ridden many times to north shore destinations. We could see such places as Luna Park (an amusement park) and Taranga Zoo, as well as Manly and Bondi beaches with the golden sand and breaking surf for which they are known.

Even though it was late in the season, there were still many sail boats out with their colorful sails blowing in the wind. Passing the Royal Botanic Garden, my mind wandered to pleasant days with my mom and grandmother walking among the beautiful, fragrant flowers. We sailed past the first, very old convict jail until finally, we passed between the heads of that beautiful natural harbor as the ship gave long, loud blasts from its horn.

We were mesmerized by the water passing swiftly below us, when Kerry said, "My uncle told me that if you breathe in as the ship rises and out as it goes down, we won't get seasick." After a few minutes, she said that maybe it was the other way around. By that time, we were hyperventilating and since we did not have motion sickness pills, it should have been no surprise that we became ill.

We were so sick that we decided to fly from Hawaii to Canada, if we were not any better after the stop in New Zealand, as our tickets had that option. Once in Auckland, stepping off the boat felt like getting off a trampoline after you have been jumping for a while. The ground felt hard, as if our feet were blocks of wood. Back on board, we were fine. A good thing as we would have to be on the water for a long time.

On our way to Fiji, the crew conducted life boat drills, which made us feel both safe and unsure. Looking at the vast expanse of the ocean was a truly awesome experience, for as far as the eye could see, there was nothing but water. As we approached the Canadian shore, not far out of Vancouver, there was a heavy fog and the huge steel compartment doors slid closed. It was kind of unnerving to realize that we could be confined between compartments. Yet, if there was a real disaster it would probably save our lives.

Getting through customs was a challenge. Just gathering our suitcases in the same spot had us chasing back and forth. We took a cab to the bus terminal and before long, we were on our way to Calgary, Alberta. As the miles rolled by, I remember the anticipation of what would lie ahead of me in Calgary. Riding through British Columbia, we would say repeatedly what a beautiful country it was with huge stands of pine trees, the likes of which we had never seen. We saw lakes that were crystal clear and mountains taller than any we could imagine.

4

FUN TIMES

———◦•◦———

WE FOUND AN APARTMENT together in a suburb of Calgary above some small stores, one of which was a drug store with a soda fountain. We had seen such places in movies but here was the real deal! We spent a lot of time there at first. Kerry and Pauline found jobs with a petroleum company. Lynette worked in retail and I found a job in a rehabilitation center. We began acclimating to our new environment, including the altitude, which left us a little sleepy at first.

Life took on the rhythm of young women becoming comfortable in their new lives and we began exploring our surroundings. We took trips to Banff National Park as well as the beautiful Lake Louise with its glacial water. We were spellbound by the thick stands of trees, rushing streams and the color of glacial water.

We also saw the Calgary Stampede, a yearly event, much like a state fair with rodeo events. Along with this was a most spectacular event by the Royal Canadian Mounted Police. Mounted on their beautiful horses, the men in their distinctive red uniforms rode at full gallop, lances forward, charging from opposite ends of the arena, missing each other by only a breath, it seemed. The spectators rising to their feet with a great roar and cheer were as impressed as we were. Funny how death-defying things can stick in your mind!

One sad day, Pauline received a phone call that her mother had died. I'll never forget the awful sound of her cry. She took the next available flight home. Lynette became homesick after about a year and Kerry married a very nice young man and went on to build a happy life. That was the end of this chapter of my life.

5

MOVING ON

———◦•◦———

Now that my friends and I had gone our separate ways, I was ready for a change. However, I was not ready to go back to Australia. After all, this was a working vacation. So, I packed up and took a bus to Salt Lake City, Utah, to sightsee and visit some acquaintances from home. My next stop would be San Francisco, California and then Sea World. This would exhaust my savings. After some work to earn more money, I planned to take the train to Vancouver, British Colombia, where there was an ocean. I had missed the ocean. I had heard a lot about how wonderful life was in that beautiful city, so both needs would be met.

As the bus pulled into the Salt Lake terminal, I was fascinated with what looked like organized chaos. Buses were arriving and departing, people scrambling for their luggage, while taxi cabs and cars lined up waiting for the new arrivals. All of this added to the thick haze of exhaust fumes that seemed to permeate everything around, leaving a thin layer of black dust along with it.

I'd planned to stay at the YWCA in Salt Lake City for a few days while I visited friends and to give me time to make further travel arrangements. I felt I would be okay financially if I stuck to my budget, saving where I could. So, the YWCA was a perfect fit. I settled into my room without unpacking much and went downstairs to socialize and to see what others were up to.

There was a large room with a television and over-stuffed chairs and sofas scattered about, much like a family room. Trying to acclimate to my new surroundings, I found a chair where I could observe what might have been protocol but after a while, I decided that there was none. Some were watching T.V., others were engrossed in conversation, while still others read or wrote letters. I decided that I would be fine.

By then I was so hungry, I was ready to eat my arm, so went in search of a fast food restaurant. I found a McDonald's restaurant a few blocks away. Purchasing a hamburger, fries and a shake, I returned to the YWCA to sit in the shade of an enormous tree. Its great branches offered protection from the hot sun, and comfort to a weary traveler.

Even though acquaintances had said to call when I got into town, I felt awkward calling them. One of them was a young man I had known in Australia. When I called, his mom said that he was working in California, but she would not hear of me staying at the YWCA. She was a gracious lady, insisting on picking me up to stay at her home for a few days.

There I was with everything I owned in a couple of suitcases in the home of a perfect stranger yet feeling very much at ease. Conversation turned to my plans for some sightseeing and my eventual relocation to Vancouver.

"My brother often goes to California on business," she said when she heard I wanted to visit there. "He might be going soon. That would save some money and would be more comfortable than a bus."

It would also lead me to a new life entirely, whether or not she knew.

6

DETOUR, WHO KNEW?

A s Mrs. Greyson had predicted, her brother was leaving the next day for California on business. Her brother, Duane, was a tall thin man, with a ready smile and a receding hairline, probably in his late thirties. He seemed nervous or preoccupied. He said he was planning to leave the next day and suggested that I stay overnight with his family while he finished up some things at his office.

We walked into the house, whereupon he said, "Monica, this is Karen, Karen this is Monica. See you honey." He left immediately after that without another word. We just looked at each other not knowing what to say. Talk about awkward!

Little did I know that would be the end of my life as I knew it. There were more people in that small home than

I had encountered at any time in my life. As I remember, there were six children, from toddler to early teen. The noise was intense and within a couple of hours, I had a headache like none other. It was claustrophobic and disorienting, but I had nowhere to go and no way to go. It was clear that Monica was uncomfortable and probably didn't appreciate having me dumped on her. We made small talk, interrupted with household disputes, as well as phone calls, and a much-needed diaper change.

After the children were in bed, the three of us sat in the front room. Duane began to explain his actions and unfold the most unlikely story I had ever heard. This family was associated with a fundamentalist group and Duane gave me some pamphlets to read, explaining the original teachings of Joseph Smith and Brigham Young regarding polygamy as the "higher law," and about those who had continued to live polygamy after the mainstream LDS church outlawed it.

Duane also claimed that for weeks before his sister's phone call, he had the feeling that there was someone he had to teach the "fullness" of the gospel to, including polygamy, but had no contacts. When the phone rang, he said to Monica this must be the person he was supposed to teach.

The next day I was on a bus to Lake Arrowhead where I spent almost a week with yet another acquaintance, reading and agonizing over the things I had been told. Had I been moved upon by God to go to Salt Lake when I did and to call my friend? Was it only coincidence that Duane was my friend's uncle? Had I really been chosen to live plural marriage as they said, and would I be damned if I didn't do it? Or was the devil after me? I was so confused, I would wake up crying. All the plans for the rest of my trip seemed unimportant now.

I returned to Salt Lake and stayed with an old roommate's aunt and uncle, continually haunted with the words I had heard about how this was from God and that I should not ignore the opportunity I was being offered.

I was feeling so disconnected and at loose ends that I called Monica and met for lunch. I had no one else to talk to. Our subsequent conversations were long and meaningful as the possibility of my being "meant" for this way of life seemed more probable.

Duane told me that polygamy was a part of Mormon church teaching was not intended to be discarded and must be kept alive by those who loved the Lord. It was a short step for me to thoughtfully consider that way of life for myself. Perhaps I romanticized the idea. There would be no reason for a woman who wanted to be married to remain single, if she had a choice in the matter.

7

BEGINNINGS OF AN UNUSUAL KIND

———◦•◦———

I BEGAN MEETING WITH SOME fundamentalists in September 1969. I had heard of plural marriage even before I joined the Mormon Church and learned more after that because of church history. I remember thinking, what if it was part of church teachings again, would I live it? The answer was that I probably would. In fact, the feeling came over me that I would do just that. I never thought of it again.

Duane and Monica took me to Sunday meetings with a large group of fundamentalists in Murray, Utah. Expecting a church building of some kind, I was surprised as we pulled into the parking lot. It was a very large piece of land, which I was told had been a farm. The original owner had died, leaving the land and buildings to one of their children. There was a small brick home and a very large metal structure which used to hold farm machinery. (In later years, the land was sold and became Fashion Place Mall, yielding a large inheritance to the owners.)

Dust swirled in the dry desert air as we drove into the parking lot. Entering through a side door, I was surprised that there were no pews. Instead, there were rows of folding chairs. There was a pulpit with folding chairs for those conducting the service.

I felt overdressed in my church clothes, as most of the women wore long, plain pioneer type dresses with their hair pulled back in a tight bun. I did not notice any jewelry, except for a plain wedding band on the women, while only a few men wore wedding bands.

The men were dressed mostly in jeans and casual shirts. Some men wore slacks with a shirt and tie. Grooming was not the greatest and the many children were poorly dressed and appeared not well cared for. Perhaps these people were poor and could not afford better clothes, but grooming costs nothing.

Seeing the many men sitting with a couple of wives or more was quite a novelty to me. Some sat with wives like ducks in a row, while others sat with a wife on each side of the man. Children were dispersed among the adults.

I'd heard of polygamy being lived a hundred years ago, but these people were telling me that it was essential to my eternal salvation now. I was fascinated with the whole affair. Much of what I was being told rang true to me, especially following long talks with Duane and Monica. They invited me to some cottage meetings where a man named Frank gave religious instruction, though they called it a genealogy class. I was on a roller coaster of emotion, at times engulfed by confusion, not knowing where to turn, but other times touched by the emotion and spirit of these people.

"Why, if polygamy was right," I asked, "wasn't the LDS church living it?"

But maybe it made sense that plural marriage could not be lived by all who would want to. God was calling people who would live this law and keep plural marriage alive, they said. Evidently, I was one of these special people. Feeling myself being swept along with all of this, I asked for a blessing of guidance.

I can imagine someone screaming, "What were you thinking?" I was such a trusting person, it didn't occur to me that I would not be told to go home!

Of course, Frank gave the blessing, in which he said that I was being given a great and unique opportunity, that it was my destiny to be there and I should never turn back as this was God's will for me. Done deal!! Things were moving very quickly. I had a great sense of urgency about it. Following the many meetings and conversations I had, I concluded that I was supposed to marry Frank, who was almost twenty years older than I was. Over the course of some of these meetings, I had been introduced to one of his wives and got to know her a little.

Having stayed in the Salt Lake area longer than I planned, I got a job in a nursing home as a nurse's aide. In those days, it was simply a matter of applying for a position. No one asked for a social security card or any other identification. I only mention this because life is different these days.

8

MOVING FAST AND OUT OF CONTROL

⸻

THE NEXT STEP WAS that I was invited to dinner to meet all of Frank's family, which was a little intimidating. It was in a modest bungalow home with a large picture window, heavily draped. An antiseptic odor met us at the door. Trying not to look past the front room, I could see the home was sparsely furnished, with two worn sofas lining two walls of the room. The walls looked in need of a fresh coat of paint and the hardwood floors needed refinishing. Beyond this, I thought, *oh my, look at all those children.*

I was introduced to Helen, who was the first wife, Nelly, whom I knew, and then Paula, who was the third wife. Then I met all the children whose names whizzed past me with no hope of return.

Helen had prepared a Mexican meal to welcome me, which I appreciated very much. I would come to learn later how difficult it must have been to come up with all the ingredients for such a nice meal. We sat at a long metal table with no tablecloth, mismatched dishes and silverware and odd chairs with torn seat covers. The children were on their best behavior, even raising their hands to be excused from the table. All were poorly dressed, and the women looked thoroughly worn out. I could see that they were not at all well off, even poor, but it was a non-issue at that point for me. This was my opportunity to show God that I would do his will.

I made the decision to marry Frank. Though I knew I was not in love in the traditional manner, I believed it would come. I was however, in love with the idea of living plural marriage. Having read some of the accounts of plural families, I suppose I romanticized the whole concept.

To make the transition from where I was staying, I moved to the Sandy home two weeks before I was married. As it turned out, I put the children out of their room, five as I remember, which they didn't seem to mind.

I was quite a novelty to some of the children, as they would gather around, chattering away. Some would watch me intently, then run off giggling. One of the little girls would stand next to me and pat my leg. I had a hard time learning their names as they resembled each other with their blue eyes and blond hair. This was all such a dramatically different experience, poles apart from all I knew. Where was my place? What was I supposed to do to fit in?

Even from Australia, my mother could tell that things

were changing but couldn't put her finger on it. Slowly I began to slip away. Fewer phone calls, less news in my letters. I enjoyed the company of my soon-to-be sister-wives. Things were cluttered, crowded, and most of the time, messy, with never ending dishes. I could see they were in poor circumstances financially, but it seemed a small price for the blessings to come. After all, I was a strong, independent, determined young woman. I could do anything I set my mind to. I believed I could help fix this. So, in I jumped!

Ultimately, it was my religious conviction that brought me to the moment that I gave myself to Frank as his fourth wife. This had come at a high price, isolating me from my family and friends as well as the church which I dearly loved. Standing there with Helen, Nelly and Paula, I felt that I was embarking on a journey that would allow me to fulfill my strongest desire: to return to my heavenly home.

My wedding night was spent in Helen's room, in her bed, but I wouldn't realize until much later that it must have been a painful experience for her. Plural wives do not have much that is their own. Their privacy and any sanctuary are among those things which are missing.

The day after I was married, I returned to work on the 11-7 shift. No one outside of Frank's family suspected that I had taken the biggest step in my life. Nelly and I worked the night shift, so we could drive together. It was partially for convenience but also because I couldn't drive a stick shift.

The time finally came when I had to drive alone. I found that it took a long time to drive from Sandy to Salt Lake in second gear. The clutch ground something awful when I tried to get into third gear. On the way home, I pulled the stick right out of the truck and had to be rescued. Nelly came to pick me up and someone towed the truck. I argued that the truck was on its last leg, but I never lived that down.

Going to work tired became a way of life as it was difficult to sleep during the day. The children were so noisy that it became almost impossible. Over the years, even though I would work 3-11, I would be so tired, it's a wonder that I didn't fall asleep at the wheel.

With the newness of getting to know the family, it took a few weeks to notice that there was no radio in the house, at least not a working one. When I lived alone, I always had music playing. It was disorienting in a way as music had been such a comfortable presence. I almost always watched the evening news and a few programs on television.

Part of my adjustment to polygamous living was that there was an absence of outside communication. The radio was full of static, making it hard to listen to and the small black and white television was only to be on when Frank was home. We were effectively cut off from the outside world. Little wonder that my sister wives at home felt so isolated. On one occasion, I accompanied Frank to a store, where there was overhead music being played. I still remember it! Anne Murray singing, "Put Your Hand in the Hand."

My goodness, I thought, *how long has it been since I've heard any kind of music?*

This was the first inclination I had that polygamous men, especially Frank, were keeping their families isolated. That, of course, did not register at the time. I would learn much later that it was part of a very effective formula used to isolate, manipulate and control their families.

In retrospect, I can see it on every hand. How could I have been so blind? Well, I was being trained to be an obedient wife. My focus in all things was to be on my husband. My life, my very being, was to revolve around him.

There would be other absences to follow, not just music, media or social times. As a family, we did not observe Christmas with gifts or even Christmas carols. I found out later that Nelly's children received gifts through Sub for Santa, but the other children did not receive gifts at all. They had no clue about Santa.

We also did not observe Easter with eggs and the like. To observe holidays in those ways was forbidden, since they were Pagan events to Frank. Thanksgiving was celebrated with all the trimmings. Someone, it seemed, always gave us a turkey. Valentine's Day was non-existent between Frank and the wives; and the children were not allowed to make Valentine cards for their mothers. We were to shun all worldly ways. We didn't really celebrate the Fourth of July. Certainly, no parades. The mothers didn't even have money to buy birthday gifts for their children, so a cake was the best we could do.

What a bland way of life without much to look forward to, especially for the children. But in some ways, we got used to it and didn't notice what we were missing.

9

SISTERS AND SISTER WIVES

Helen and Nelly were sisters from the same parents. Blood sisters marrying the same man doesn't happen very often and I think perhaps it was the cause of some differences between them.

Helen was a sweet, simple soul; kind, generous and trusting, trying to fill her role of first wife. She was the legal wife, hence the title of first wife. It was hard for her to keep her thoughts straight. She often got things mixed up and could be very forgetful especially when time was involved. It didn't take much to make Helen happy; just a smile or a thank you would be enough. When she was frustrated or embarrassed, she would say, "Oh, gab." Whatever that meant, it was a signature phrase.

She should have met some kind man, even if in polygamy, who would love her for her innocence. It would have been better for Helen if Frank had never insisted on having so many children, rather than having two or three. She needed protection from the unkind world around her. The hardship she endured took a major toll on her physical and mental health.

Frank would say demeaning things to her such as, "You don't know what you are talking about. You never get things right." And she didn't, but who says those kinds of things to a sweet, loving wife? She believed in him when few others did, was easily pleased and thought that the things that happened in the bedroom meant he loved and cherished her.

Her sense of self-worth came from the number of children she gave birth to. While Helen was living out of town and I was still working in Salt Lake, I received a letter from her in which she said, "Not much to say, we are fine, everything is the same. I am trying to learn to be the wife and mother I desire to be. Maybe now I can get something done right. I will be the happiest woman in the world when I don't have to hear 'I can't understand you' anymore (from Frank)."

Helen was always rearranging the furniture, which was the only thing she had any control over. It could be dangerous to come home from work at night in the dark, as you could fall over something that wasn't there earlier in the day. Sleep became a refuge for her. She was the first person I'd known who was waiting to die. That was the only way out for her.

Nelly was also very insecure. Her childhood had taught her to hide her true self and had created a facade of confidence that seemed to fill her need to be the wife Frank could trust to do things right. She also had the ability to believe the things she told herself until they became reality to her. We used to mark our diapers, socks and undershirts, small items such as those with a dot of embroidery floss. We did this as we could not rely on size alone to tell what clothing belonged to which mother's children. Mine was green. One-time Nelly argued vigorously, relentlessly that the dot on a pair of socks was blue. She became very distressed and I gave up, it wasn't worth the struggle.

Nelly also found self-worth in the number of children she gave birth to but didn't seem to want to nurture them. It took a long time for me to figure this out. I never felt comfortable with Nelly. It also took a while for me to realize there were discrepancies in things she told me. Such as a conversation between herself and Paula, which she told in at least two different versions. I called her on it once but never did it again. The consequences were too severe.

I could not risk confiding in Nelly, as she would have no qualms about changing my words, then use them to her advantage. She would play her children against the other mothers and could create quite a mess. Their personalities were so different, Helen and Nelly, that I asked once how they ended up married to the same man. Apparently, after Helen and Frank were married, her father told Frank that he had another daughter for him to marry, who was Nelly, and that was that.

Paula was young, not fifteen as you might be thinking, but still younger than the others. She was quiet and gentle. It took a lot to make her angry, but when she was, *take cover!*

To me, Paula seemed to be the voice of reason. Now, I can see that she was trying to find her way in this unusual mix of personalities.

A few months after I was married, she wrote a very sweet letter assuring me that everything would get easier with time. Out of respect to her, I will not offer any of her familial information. She was however, "in hiding," which meant that she was forced to continually remain in the house with the curtains drawn. I felt sorry for her as we were the only people she had contact with. On the rare occasion she did leave, it was under the cover of darkness. Talk about stir crazy! I don't know how she handled being kept hidden for so long.

As the years passed, Frank took two more wives, each with our collective consent. The first of these was Grace, an older woman, hard-working and kind. The other, Betty was in her mid-thirties. Grace's children were grown and had families of their own. Frank took advantage of her work ethic, sending her to live with sister-wives who need-ed help learning how to keep a home clean and running smoothly. It could not have been easy for her, as many of the children treated her as a servant.

Betty was hard for me to understand as she was educat-ed but unwilling to go to work to help the family. She was not able to have children and I wondered if she felt that it was not her problem. Perhaps staying home was a way to remain near Frank.

In later years, Grace and Betty lived in the "Yellow house," which was a beautiful old home at one time. It was probably built in the early nineteen hundreds with ornate woodwork and gingerbread cookie finish to the front of the upstairs outside wall.

A neighbor told me that it also had an ornate front porch which someone removed during a time when the house was unoccupied. There was a bay window with leaded colored windows which allowed sunlight to fill the room. That was the front room which had tall pocket doors which lead into the dining room that led into a very small kitchen. The ceilings were very high as many were in that period. A winding stairway of heavy wood led to the second floor. All the wood was heavy dark wood, lending a richness to the home.

There were four bedrooms upstairs with an open space for a sitting room which had a gas space heater in a corner. There was a stairway leading downstairs to a small foyer, another small room off to the side then the front door. Many of the windows had colored glass on the top part with clear glass on the lower two thirds. There was only one working bathroom and Frank had a wood burning stove installed just off the kitchen for heat. It was another of my lovely old homes, if only we could restore it to its original splendor.

The name "Yellow house" came from some yellow curtains I had made for another home and gave to the mothers living there. Frank would put as many of our mothers and their children into one home as possible, I suppose to save money. At one time, Nelly and six of her children lived with Grace and Betty in that home. The children were not allowed outside to play so all were trapped in there together. Frank made the downstairs room into his office and soon closed off the front stairs, so the children could not go down and interrupt him also to keep the noise upstairs.

Downstairs was also where Frank's library was housed. Rooms were added but never finished to reasonable living standards, but it didn't affect him in the least. The back porch was framed in for, what else but books.

Betty worked in Frank's library, organizing and cataloging in general. She supported Frank's choice to remain unemployed. Grace remained the housekeeper and confided to me that she felt that she was only good for cleaning toilets.

Beyond thinking that he had a responsibility to write the history of "the work," that is polygamy after the manifesto, Frank had long since settled into a life of unemployment. He attempted to make this into a noble thing by taking a scripture out of context which talks about the laborer in Zion. It states the laborer in Zion shall labor for Zion, for if they labor for money they shall perish. Frank was able to twist this scripture to suit his desire not to work. Evidently, it was all right for his wives to perish, just so long as he did not. Once there was no money coming in, after Grace died and her social security money stopped, Betty finally went to work to support the two of them. What goes around comes around, I suppose.

Frank was from a broken home, at times being placed in foster care. His mother would visit him occasionally, now and then telling him that she would pick him up for a birthday or for Christmas, only to leave him to wonder why she didn't come and where she was. It must have been devastating for a little boy to feel abandoned.

At some point, he was reunited with his mother and younger brother. These were hard times for everyone financially and emotionally. He told of pulling a cart around selling cookies and aprons to help his mom. His mom would praise him if he could wear his clothes all week without getting them dirty. I wish she hadn't, as none of his wives could convince him that it was nearly impossible to get the cuffs and collars of the white shirts he insisted on wearing for so long, clean.

Frank had habits that had been with him for a lifetime, at least to this point. His mother must have been a strong influence as far as hygiene was concerned. Curbing utility costs and the like stuck with him. Once weekly baths with washing up in between was his norm. The wives were to follow suit but I know I cheated!

He wore the same pair of dark pants and white shirt every day of the week. We could not convince him to change his shirts. He heard that deodorant caused cancer, so no one else could use deodorant. Moreover, toothpaste, he said, had fluoride in it. He had read something about fluoride making a person's flesh fall of their bones. We could only use baking soda. Yuck!

Frank had some mind-numbing habits. Not that I don't have my own, but this is about him! He carried a small spiral note book in which he would write everything he needed to remember. Not that it was a bad idea, he just made such a big deal out of it. He also kept a sharpened, to a point, pencil in his shirt pocket. Men in the Order would ask to borrow his pencil so he took to keeping three or four pencils in his pocket. I think the men were making fun of him, but he didn't catch on. Took it all seriously. He wouldn't have appreciated it if he had. He would not have appreciated the humor at his expense. He couldn't laugh at himself. He took some things too seriously, some not seriously enough.

One day, as I was leaving, I reached around his shoulder to say goodbye when one of those pencils almost poked me in the eye. I pulled back abruptly, exclaiming that it almost got me. He was so angry that he pushed me away. I guess he saw it as a criticism. It was another one of those, *What just happened?* moments.

Another mind-bending habit was that Frank liked to plan things to the smallest detail. I tend to run on generalities and what is right in front of me. Unfortunately, most of these plans were not practical in the real world and never came to fruition.

We had a station wagon at one time which was in constant use for the entire family. Frank literally spent days making a chart scheduling every destination for every driver every minute the vehicle was to be used. Coming up with the money to run the vehicle was a constant issue. He would give us a couple of dollars at a time, which didn't go far.

When Frank first came into the group, the leader Mr. Fisher advised him to, "go ahead and enter plural marriage as the Lord would provide." This is a good point, but I think you must be realistic and do your part.

At the time, Frank was paying for a home for Gloria, who had divorced him, and Helen. Frank would have done well as an academic as he was very smart but had no aptitude for financial things, not even the most basic. He was hopeless and took advice from the man who became his mentor, who also did not have a head for even the most ordinary things of life. To his death, Frank remained devoted to Mr. Fisher believing he was the only one to whom he would be accountable. Frank truly believed that he would be vindicated in his actions.

Polygamists can't afford to be extravagant. Nevertheless, as Frank's financial circumstances grew worse as the number of children increased, the family really did become poor. Not only financially, but mentally as we could see no other way. Frank liked that we looked the part—worn out clothing, tattered shoes and living out of dumpsters. He managed to flip this into something to be proud of and how anyone who is humble enough would be pleased to live.

There is a level of human dignity that requires a person to pull their weight, pay their way, not be a drain on others, and to be clean and comely within their means. But Frank thrust us so far below that standard that we could not see our way past the poverty mentality.

People would give us their worn out clothing and other old things they didn't want. Someone gave us a barrel of odd socks, which we spent months trying to pair up. Another man gave us some of his old food storage, which was kind enough, but this was old! It included large bags of raisins, which was something we never had the opportunity to buy and never found in the bins. After tearing one open we found there were weevils all through it. I have heard that weevils are a good source of protein, and that prisoners of war would eat them to survive, but we were not prisoners of war.

Or were we? Frank was very pleased with us as we worked through those weevil-infested raisins, washing them off and using them in different ways. We were certainly appreciative enough but wondered if people felt obliged to try to help us not only because our need was so openly displayed but that Frank was on the council.

To shun the very appearance of secular life made it easier for him to withdraw into his own sense of reality, immersing himself in his books, becoming oblivious to his family's struggles. It was a sticky web he was weaving.

10

WALKING INTO PLURAL MARRIAGE ...

Walking into plural marriage without first seeing it lived can be hazardous to your sense of self-worth. It should not have been a surprise, launching into an entirely different way of life, but it was. My mother would have said that I never looked before I leaped into pretty much anything, always running on emotion and adrenaline. I think she would be right.

I have heard that women tend to "marry their father." In retrospect, I think that there was some of that transference in my head. Some self-defeating sensor subconsciously told me that I would get what I thought I deserved: a defeating male dominance. Frank's rule was absolute and from a safe distance for him, rarely interacting with the family, but in control.

He saw women as inferior. He was gifted with words and used them skillfully, saying such things as, "Just as the head is superior to the rest of the body, the man is the head and has the intellect and governs his family; the woman works as the rest of the body does." At times this was blatantly stated and sometimes it was subtle, though always effective. If Frank had ever been confronted on his views on women or his choice of words, which I never did, I am confident that he would have put it in anatomical terms, thus avoiding revealing his true intention.

Frank had become a member of the LDS church in his late twenties, met and married a woman a little his senior. While learning about church history, he came upon the practice of plural marriage, which evidently intrigued him. There was a co-worker, Mr. Ebeye, with whom he would discuss the things he was learning. Mr. Ebeye never became involved but introduced him to some polygamists who were meeting in the valley.

Frank was one of those people who would focus on a religious extreme, taking a tidbit of something he learned and then become fanatical about it. Even though the Church of Jesus Christ of Latter-day Saints did not at the time—and does not currently—practice polygamy, Frank had other ideas about that. Gloria was Frank's wife at the time and was quite the proper southern lady. When he went home with the news that he had met a young lady whom he intended to marry, thus entering polygamy, she replied, "The hell you are. Get out of my house!"

She filed for divorce, as she would have nothing to do with it. Forty years later, and dying of cancer, we convinced her to come to the yellow house where she could be taken care of until her death.

When I first married Frank, he was a technical writer for a large publishing company located north of Salt Lake City which was a long commute for him. He was very smart and could have obtained an education and been in some profession, but for reasons only he knew, never went to school. His position involved training employees with a degree to do a part of their job within the company. He seemed to resent that and would demean the education they had to us, saying that it was only a piece of paper; completely missing the point of that degree.

Our children were never encouraged to seek higher education. In fact, they were lucky to get through high school. His reasoning was that public schools and universities would corrupt the children's minds and pull them away from "the Work," that being our religious belief. What was odd to me, was that on more than one occasion, Frank said that a child should never make more than his father did. It didn't even make sense; it was so unrealistic. Did he even think about what he was saying?

Nelly and I worked as nurse's aides, which were not high paying jobs, but we had to help some. We signed our paychecks over to Frank, feeling this was an equitable arrangement as we were committed to working for the good of the whole. Helen and Paula tended the children and did the most part of the household chores. There was no personal spending money. If we needed something, Frank provided the specific item. Everything came through Frank, what little there was.

In the fall of 1968, I was working for a staffing agency and was sent regularly to Pioneer Valley Hospital. They liked my work and offered to send me to school to become a Licensed Practical Nurse, with a contract to work for them for two years following graduation. Ecstatic, I brought this up at the next family council but was shot down as Nelly was supposed to be our family nurse. I was angry and disappointed. I had no children at the time and it would have been perfect timing. Next thing I knew, Nelly was enrolled at the community college for the same course I had been offered.

This was just the beginning of the family being at the mercy of Nelly's demands and it deepened the chasm forming between us. Her tantrums dictated how the family ran until the death of her father, who was at the time, the head of the group, and Frank's father-in-law. She went on to live in her own rented homes, expecting Frank to finance her whenever she felt like it. Honey soon turned to vinegar.

11

LIFE ON THE HOME FRONT

⸺◦•◦⸺

NOT EVERYTHING WAS TERRIBLE. The camaraderie between sister wives from time to time was quite pleasant. At one time, Helen, Nelly, Paula and I had babies close to each other. They were affectionately known as the quads.

Imagine being a mother at home with the babies in their high chairs lined up much like baby birds. Bibs on, bowl of cereal in one hand, a spoon in the other moving along the line until all were fed. Just like an assembly line.

Then there was the diaper changing assembly line. Armed with a stack of cloth diapers, it was a matter of catch and release. Quite the workout, which required practice before mastering the process.

Nap time was not quite the assembly line process. There were four babies, four bottles, three cribs and one poorly constructed play pen. The quads were pretty much mobile at this time. One beautiful day, all was quiet when suddenly one of them slipped out of the play pen and took off joyfully free. Who can get four babies to sleep at the same time? Not me!

Frank advocated the concept of a generic mother. That meant we were to love and care for each other's children as if we had given birth to them ourselves. It was as if he didn't want the children to have a special relationship with their own birth mother. Over the years, all the children felt free to go to one mother or another for care or comfort. But I felt that I could not meet Frank's expectations. I think that when you carry a baby under your heart for nine months, then give birth to that child, there is an inexplicable bond that can never be broken or equaled.

12

PRIDE

———◦•◦———

WE CAN TAKE PRIDE in many things, for example: a good job well done, our children's accomplishments, or our wonderful country. Frank took pride in being poor. We looked the part. For some reason, he equated being poor with being righteous and humble.

There is an unwritten rule in plural marriage, that a man governs his family, making sure he is obeyed. Frank used to say that when you have one wife, it is easy to keep her under your thumb, two wives you must use both hands. There was no such thing as working out differing opinions, as he would say that he knew the overall needs of the family so that was the end of it.

I was frequently reminded that I had not grown up in the Work and needed to learn my role in the family. I needed to learn my role as a woman. I took this to heart because I was committed to living plural marriage and wanted to live it to the very best of my ability. Being so open and trying to learn seems not to have served me well. I accepted everything Frank and Nelly told me to correct my ways. Frank definitely had the need to control, though I did not see it for many years.

Women were to be subjugated and ruled over. As he would say, "It's a man's world." He believed that it gave him license to disregard his wives. His view was so skewed that he was ultimately unable to see any other way. Sadly, he increasingly continued to distance his wives, and more particularly his children. He did this by simply not being at home until the children were in bed and not being available to his wives when he was home, spending time in his library. No social time interacting with each other, definitely no date night.

In the group at large, women were not physically abused to my knowledge. Instead, they were mentally controlled.

It was a common theme in church meetings to hear one man or another belittle one wife or another—mercifully only rarely using her name. They would say such things as, "Well, you have a couple of wives saying that they want to live in the same house together, but you put them off until they are begging you because they don't really know what they want, and will usually change their minds. They never know what they want." I hated that. Women were told that their purpose in this life was to bear children and raise them to perpetuate plural marriage. "Raising up a righteous seed," it was called. We were told that a wife must obey her husband in all things and to please him. A wife must teach her children to do as their father wants them to do. A wife must not have friends outside of her family. A man must never allow a wife to know his financial affairs although she could work outside of the home to help support the family.

Speakers in Sunday meetings were never assigned beforehand. As a rule, a council member would conduct the meeting addressing some issue or another, but usually that of women obeying their husband and for the men to follow the council members. *Wow, obedience for men.* It was kind of a disciplinary affair for the most part, with very rare emphasis on the Savior. Once in a great while, one of them would bring up the concept of Christ-like behavior. Mostly, it was the issue of obedience. Any other speakers were called upon to "speak by the spirit" right on the spot.

Such extemporaneous speaking was a terrifying event and I only did it once in my thirty-five years of polygamist life. It would be wise to have something rattling around in your head though, just in case. One man whom I really did respect, the employed kind who took care of his families, was very familiar with scripture, especially the *Book of Mormon.* I loved it when he spoke, as he taught gospel principles and always directed us toward Jesus. It was most refreshing.

Another favorite topic, especially from council members, was that of being fair. Many a tirade came over the pulpit degrading women who expressed the idea of something being unfair, so often making them sound like petulant children.

Wives could have used different words to more accurately define their views or needs but trying to express your feelings was not something which was encouraged. To have your thoughts constantly dismissed as being trivial and unwanted takes a toll.

When I was a new wife, I constantly tested the waters to ascertain the correct way of going about everyday living. I later found that it was not at all unusual for new wives to have to figure that out. Being demeaned in these many ways took the sparkle out of life and tested my dedication to live plural marriage.

The heavy correction came from people I was supposed to trust, leaders who, as it turned out, could hardly hold their own families together. The other men, like my husband, rarely held jobs and were poor examples to their children. It didn't take long to wonder what I had gotten myself into. *How does one deal with these contradictions?*

Let me tell you what happens. You buy into it. To mentally and emotionally survive, as irrational as it sounds, you become that mindless appendage. You relinquish your true self to become what your husband says you must be. More than once, our husband told us that a man is only required to love a woman as much as she is obedient to him.

On one occasion, Frank told me that his disapproval was his only defense against his family. What a tragic place he had come to in life. He saw himself as some superior being who ruled with his powerful disapproval. It was clear, whether innate or something he learned, he believed that as a man living plural marriage, he was most definitely superior to any woman. And this was supposed to be a religious-based way of life.

Once, I took a chance and reminded Frank that Jesus said, 'He who was the greatest of all, was the servant of all.' In the Bible, it is in reference to the Savior, but I was thinking more along the line of serving each other as husband and wife. You know, considerate and caring, doing little things you know the other will appreciate. It was not a good choice to question him like this. I could feel the barrier rising between us.

His reply was to the effect of, "Well what am I to do? Should I go to each wife and ask, 'What can I do for you dear?' and so on?" He could say things in the most belittling way. His message was absolutely clear: that it was the wife's duty to learn what her husband wanted her to do and do it. What a sterile environment it was, keeping an impenetrable barrier between husband and wife.

A nebulous cloud of threat hung almost constantly over the group, as the council members seemed to have the need to keep people guessing as to whether they were worthy. Either in their eyes or in the eyes of God, it was never clear. So often, it felt like doom, with no clear way to measure myself. I would feel so fearful. There was no yardstick, except to be obedient to my husband. There were only endless words, leaving nothing but confusion and the desired amount of control that flowed from the pulpit.

One of the most disturbing sermons I heard was that of how the women must place their hearts on the altar, allow them to be broken so that they could be useful. Before polygamy, I had heard of giving one's heart to God, but the way this sermon was delivered left me wondering if the speaker meant on God's altar or their husband's.

Have you ever watched a storm move across the sky, dark heavy clouds, with rolling thunder, air almost static with the building of ionization? That is how I felt, always waiting for the lightning to strike, never knowing if I was acceptable to God or if my children and I were safe.

Even though everywhere I looked, there seemed to be close, loving families and sister-wives, the opposite was also clearly noticeable. I would see a woman with sadness so heavy that she need not speak, her eyes as lifeless as mine were becoming. There were more women like this than I had ever imagined before living amongst them.

Even as a proponent of plural marriage, sooner or later you realize that there are a multitude of emotions and feelings present. Swirling loosely at first on the surface, these emotions become a whirlpool, spiraling deeper into the psyche, inevitably damaging the family. Women are told to overcome their weaknesses and then left to make their marriages work, as if their husbands were not part of the equation. This defied reason to me. I wondered if the men were just ill-prepared as they took more wives. Perhaps they became overwhelmed and it was easier to put the burden onto the wife.

13

NEW TERRITORY

───◦•◦───

I HAD A STEEP LEARNING curve as I integrated into a culture that was so foreign to me. I learned quickly that a wife was to be seen and not heard, she's not to think for herself and she's never allowed emotion. She must obey, smile, say "yes, dear" and provide many children for her husband. Never were we to question our husband's decisions nor even to entertain the concept of working anything out with them, as that was closely akin to complaining. If I was so bold as to try, I was quickly pulled into line with the dreaded yet inevitable accusation that I was being emotional, or worse, jealous.

No matter the difficulty or concern, I could count on the same unwavering answer: that there would be no change because I did not see the overall needs of the family, followed by deafening silence. Should any of us be desperate enough to find our own solution and dare to take action, we would have been pronounced to be the lowest of all disobedient wives, "a law unto yourself." This judgment was like having cold water dumped on you, both shocking and humiliating.

In retrospect, and with the benefit of some experience, I can see that it was just easier for the polygamous men to flex their manly "I'm in charge muscles" to avoid dealing with family issues. For some, this tactic would come back to bite them; for some it would serve them well, but it was always the complaining woman who was criticized, sentenced and condemned. Women were taught that they were to be obedient to their husbands at the peril of their salvation.

I remember hearing one man say that he felt sorry for women as they had so much to learn, which, for about a second, sounded all right, but I couldn't help wondering if he knew that the men had a lot to learn, as well. Polygamy attracts the type of men who do not wish to be accountable to anyone, least of all their wives. Marriage was not a partnership.

Later in my marriage, when I had found some gumption, I expressed to Frank the sense of a woman being hopelessly trapped in a marriage where she had no autonomy, no sense of self, consumed with despair. He replied to the effect that God would remove such a husband. I replied that would not happen in this life, so in reality, she had no hope.

He may have been surprised by that. It certainly was a warning of things to come when I would ask for a release. In the meantime, I said a lot of "yes, dears."

14

OBSERVATIONS

———◦•◦———

THOUGHTS BEGAN TO SWIRL in my mind as I considered what I was feeling and experiencing in polygamy at this point. I was remarkably unaware of how other families faired. What was family life like for them? I had never seen plural marriage lived, knowing only what Frank told me. I was clueless as to how other women coped. What were their true inner feelings about it?

What I did know was that if a woman was foolish enough to speak to a council member for advice, she would soon find that it was not a confidence between them as the husband would be informed of their conversation. In most religions, members can seek guidance from their minister or pastor. These conversations are never disclosed and are private. Not so in the group. She would be sent home to pray for her husband and then take the backlash of seeking advice from someone other than her husband.

I grew to value the friendship of a couple of women my age in our group. These women never spoke badly of their husbands and openly exhibited loyalty toward them. But they had, to some degree or another, relinquished emotional attachment to them. I respected the dignity they exhibited, using their example to hold on as long as I could.

They had found a way to endure, enjoying their friendship as they continued to live out their lives. I feel it is important to say that they were among the few I saw who were focused on the Savior. He was their mainstay.

But for the rest of us, we were told our husband was to be our mainstay. That seemed to be the only secret for survival: give lip service to your husband and hang on for dear life. Most of us muddled around, trying to figure out how to survive, how to figure out what our husbands wanted and then to accomplish it. All hope and trust was to reside in the husband.

My sister wives and I were taught that our husband was our head, and that he was the only one we were to look to for guidance and instruction. He was the one we would go through to get to the Savior and God. I have no doubt that the majority of the men held the same view.

One of my sister wives, who is now deceased, confided to me that one night before going to bed, she was praying and Frank asked her what she was doing. She replied that she was praying. His response was that her husband was there, why did she need to pray? It didn't sit right at the time and seems even more ludicrous now.

15

GREENS A.K.A. DUMPSTER DIVING

I USED TO THINK THAT someday I would write a book and title it "Do You Have Any Boxes?" This came from the years of dumpster diving. We called it going for greens, which I did to obtain food for our ever-expanding family and eventually Order families, which were families who became affiliated with Frank and our family.

I had a driving route for my dumpster diving that has become completely blurred in my memory even though I sometimes dream about it. In the dream, nothing seems right, and I awake grateful that it was only a dream. In reality, sleep would not take away my fears so easily.

I would start right after six a.m. prayers, usually on a Monday, leaving my children to be taken care of by a sister wife. Then, driving from one dumpster to another dumpster, I found that I was not the only one looking for food. Some people were there for their own personal use, and some for their animals. Competition could be tough, and there was dumpster etiquette. If I should pull up and someone was already working through the bin, it was only polite to ask if it was okay to look through the bins as well.

My first time doing this, I was nervous, afraid that someone would discover me and have me arrested for trespassing. The thing that made this bearable was turning it into a game. To see if I could be the first person to that bin seemed to help and took the edge off.

Sometimes there would be boxes (the size of a banana box) of produce stacked on the loading dock, which made it easier for me. Before compacters, there were bins taller than me, with a ledge on two sides where the garbage truck would lift the bin to empty the contents. It was this ledge that I would climb onto to reach into the bin. It also gave me footing from which I could climb to the top of the bin and jump in to retrieve food. The trick was to make sure there were enough solid looking boxes to climb onto to get back out.

Unfortunately, these were commercial bins and I'm sure they were never washed out, so the odor was pretty much overwhelming any time of year but especially during the hot months. Adding to the nastiness of the bins was the fact that some employees would split open the containers of milk, so it would spill out, or hurl cartons of cottage cheese or yogurt so they would splatter all over the inside of the bin.

Sometimes the food would be largely intact and in I would go, filling one box at a time, carefully lifting it and balancing it on the corner of the bin so it would not tip back inside, which happened every so often. Then I would climb out and carefully lift the box down and into what-ever vehicle I was using that day, repeating the process as many times as needed. This was an especially difficult task when I was pregnant.

Occasionally, I would take one or two of my children with me when school was out, so I could spend time with them. There were even times when I was still in a dumpster bin and the garbage truck would pull up. I would pop my head up and ask for a few minutes to finish getting my haul out. Some drivers were patient with me while others were not, and the children would start crying, thinking that I would end up in the dump truck. If we were lucky, the produce would be in good condition and occasionally I would find good dairy and bread items. We would clean up what I brought home and use it as best we could.

Through it all, I didn't begrudge my assigned task as procurer of questionable food. We would always say a prayer over our meals and no one ever got sick from them. Our family lived on what I was able to gather from those trips, and we were grateful. However, the Order families fared better than we did since they could purchase some of the things we didn't find in the greens. For our children, there was little to no milk or juice in the fridge, very little fresh fruit and even less protein in their diets.

There would be times when I'd dig around in the bins and a store employee would come out to toss something away. There would be an awkward moment. Trying to ap-pear nonchalant, I would say, "Do you have any boxes?" but I knew I wasn't fooling anyone. It was an attempt to obtain some dignity and avoid the feelings of shame.

There were some dark days during the dumpster era. It was clear that our husband was not concerned about our well-being or what we had to do to survive. I felt very much alone, though I was surrounded by people. This is when I realized that depression was a very real thing and that hopelessness had become a constant companion. I felt so responsible for feeding the family!

There was one produce manager who was very considerate of my predicament. I think he had me figured out from the beginning, but he was always kind. On one of those truly dark days, this kind man from the store put his hand on my shoulder and said, "Don't worry, I'll take care of you." Those words touched me so very deeply.

Of course, he was referring to produce, but it struck me so profoundly that my own husband had never spoken those words to me, nor anything like it. Yet, here was a good and generous man who had no responsibility toward me. Many years later, when I was able to purchase food, I would still smell the newly opened milk and taste it to be sure it was still good. Old habits die hard!

16

LIONS AND TIGERS
AND BEARS, *OH MY!*

IN THE EARLY DAYS, our family went to a naturopathic doctor for our medical and birthing needs. He was a wonderful man. He was gentle, kind and well respected in the medical community. His practice included people from many walks of life. I think he also operated in the red, as no one was turned away from his care. Many of his patients were plural families—which meant home births, some of which went unpaid, including my own family. He was the epitome of the old country doctor, always available and would go to a home any time, and in any weather.

Dr. Allred was murdered in his office, one dreadful day, shot by a woman sent by a rival polygamist leader. The investigation was led by a police detective with whom I would become acquainted thirty years later. Life swings on very small hinges!

It was May 1977 and I was pregnant with my fourth child. The shock and grief were palpable. No one seemed to know what to do. It was as if a big chunk of our hearts were missing, big enough to drive a truck through. He delivered my first three babies and I was carrying my fourth baby when he died. Along with the sense of loss came the question of who would deliver the baby I was carrying.

Frank decided that Nelly was to be our family midwife from that time on, which was not great news for me. Nelly and I did not get along at all and she had no experience as a midwife. Would she know what to do if the birth was complicated? And how could I share such a personal, even spiritual experience, with her? Good thing my little girl was in a hurry to be born and came without incident as this was Nelly's first experience.

Dr. Allred had also seen me through scarlet fever and chicken pox. The only childhood illness I had was the measles and I hadn't been immunized. I was so sick with scarlet fever and such a mess with chicken pox. Eight months pregnant and covered with pustules, which were almost impossible not to scratch. That boy never did catch chicken pox!

This brings me to an unusual way of thinking. Our husband would not allow us to have our children immunized. He was shocked when I brought it up. According to him, it didn't serve any purpose except for the government to keep track of us. This underlying current of fear was perpetuated endlessly throughout the group. Some were more engulfed in it than others, but we were in the lead. It was widespread.

The polygamist group at large was skeptical of medical doctors and fearful of hospitals. It was all right to resort to doctors and hospitals if you were in dire need, but it was a kind of condescension to allow their intervention even then, and perpetuating a bad reputation meant it was easier to expect charity to cover the costs.

There were horror stories circulating about hospitals putting tracking devices in babies' heads during delivery, which fanned the fire of distrust. Homebirths were expected of the women, while those who went to a hospital were looked upon as less faithful, not living your religion sort of thing. Adding to the pressure, I heard one man who championed the idea that women who had their babies at home clearly loved their children more than those who did not. Almost no one had health insurance, and Frank justified this by saying we should simply use our faith to be healed.

Perhaps I didn't have enough, but sometimes we need outside help!

Another thing we were not permitted to do was to legally register the births of our children. I can see looking back that this was yet another fear tactic, to keep us in line while remaining under the cloak of secrecy. Frank really thought we should be invisible to the government. But if push had ever come to shove, the mothers could not have proven that their children were theirs. That worked for Frank, because then he could never be accused of neglecting any of us, because we weren't legally his.

Looking back, the image I see now of the wives is that of frightened little mice, scurrying about, scarcely knowing which way to turn, always nervous of any shadow that might fall across our path. We were always watching to see if perhaps a car was parked outside our home, wondering if we were under surveillance by the government. Our curtains were always drawn, and our children were kept in the house while chaos reigned, never feeling the joy of the sun on their faces while playing in the fresh air.

All of this affected us and wore on the very fabric of my life. I was often screaming inside for the want of normalcy; to be as I used to be, free and unafraid.

Frank seemed to think that however he saw things, that was how they were. Nothing could dissuade him from it. He had no place for reality. He had been told several times by his father-in-law, Mr. Anderson, who also happened to be the leader of the group, to get birth certificates for our children. But Frank refused. A sad commentary, as Frank would not take much needed guidance from someone who had a vested interest and a sincere desire to help him succeed. Mr. Anderson was just trying to show Frank how to show love and gain the confidence of his wives. Frank told this man, the father of two of Frank's wives, that he didn't tell him how to rule his family, so his father-in-law didn't need to tell him how to rule his. We were not preparing our children to live and function in everyday life.

———

FOR OUR FAMILY, THERE were no well child checkups with a pediatrician, no checkups with a dentist. In fact, a child would have to have a bad toothache before Frank would allow us to take him to the dentist. The dentist we went to was across the street from Dr. Allred's office. He was a kindly man, who never asked questions and never asked the accompanying mother for payment. I often wondered if he was ever paid in full. There must be a special place in heaven for men like him.

Recently, I stopped by this dentist's office to thank him for his past kindness. He told me that he couldn't let children go without helping them. He had been battling cancer at the time and I have since heard of his death. I am so glad that I was able to speak with him when I did.

I remember one of Helen's little girls had fallen off a bike and was in a lot of pain. Later in the afternoon, Nelly sent me with the little girl to the emergency room. She had a broken arm and it had to be casted.

As I drove home into the yard, I was greeted by Frank yelling, "I can't believe you did this." I couldn't believe he was angry at me for taking his daughter to the hospital. By this time, Dr. Allred had been killed and we had no one else to go to but the hospital.

One of my boys was an accident looking to happen. While playing with a friend who owned a BB gun, my son was convinced to catch the pellet as it came out of the barrel, which he tried, only to have it lodge in the web of his hand. I had to take him to urgent care to have it dug out. That would not be the last time I would be chastised for taking a child to urgent care, but what do you do?

This same child, while playing, inhaled a dried pea. I don't know why he had it in his mouth to begin with, but he did. At first, he said that he had swallowed it and I told him not to worry as it would come out the other end. He continued to play, but by evening he was coughing hard.

Around one in the morning his cough was so much

worse. That is when he said that it gone down his wind pipe. Now I was worried, so I took him to the emergency room to be checked out. An x-ray revealed nothing, and the doctors concluded that he really had swallowed the pea and that his throat was sore from coughing. They gave him a "G.I." (gastro-intestinal) cocktail, a mix of soothing ingredients, and sent us home.

Days passed, and he looked awful, perspiring and coughing so hard he would gag. To say that Frank was angry about the debt I had incurred would be an under-statement. He encouraged my son to have faith that he would be healed.

But when I returned from work the next evening, it was clear that my boy was in serious trouble—his heart hammering, his face red and his body wet with perspi-ration. Just as I scooped him up to take him back to the hospital, he coughed up one half of a fully hydrated pea with the beginning of a shoot attached to it, including the outer casing. It had actually begun to grow inside of him!

After a couple more coughs, out came the other half. I was tempted to take it back to the hospital to show them they'd been wrong, but I knew that I couldn't prove what had happened. Besides, what would be the point? His re-covery was complete, except for getting winded when he exerted himself. To this day, he wheezes with exertion. Frank felt vindicated in his thinking, though he didn't know how close I came to disobeying him again and re-turning to the hospital.

About thirty years ago, there was an outbreak of hepa-titis in the group and some of our family became very ill.

True to form, no medical help was sought. All eventually recovered, but I think one of the mothers had some liver damage. We were ridiculed if we wanted to see a doctor for some reason or another. Frank would say condescendingly, "It helps to put a name on it," as if the only thing that mattered to us was having a diagnosis—not the cure. He knew exactly how to make us feel foolish.

Most of the health problems resolved naturally, but that wasn't true of Grace. Grace had heart trouble most of her adult life which worsened with age and hard work. Her health declined due to her refusing to see a doctor as she clung to Frank's opinion about not seeking medical care. There were two doctors in the group by that time, but with a lifetime of seeing obedience as a measure of faithfulness to her husband and therefore to God, she continued to go downhill.

Eventually she became bedridden and was moved from her room upstairs with its years of familiarity, only to be warehoused in a tiny, unfinished, un-insulated, windowless room. It was freezing cold in the winter and sweltering in the summer, surrounded by walls of bookshelves filled with Frank's journals. Grace's own children were not welcomed to see their mother and for good reason: Frank didn't want to deal with their complaints about their mother's care.

One of Grace's daughters who lived nearby was finally able to get in to see her and was appalled to see how poorly she was being taken care of, while Frank remained safely cloistered in his office. Months later, the daughter and her husband came in and picked Grace up, taking her to their home. Grace was so conflicted, as she was torn between the care of her family and the disapproval of her husband. Frank insisted that his wife had been kidnapped. Reluctantly, Grace was returned to die in isolated seclusion from those who loved her, all in the name of obedience.

17

HOMESCHOOL

———⊃◆⊂———

F RANK BELIEVED THAT THE public-school system would destroy our children emotionally as well as spiritually, so along with our shrouded life came homeschool. It all began with Helen's four oldest. Two of them came home from school with consent forms for a sex education class. Frank was adamantly opposed to the school addressing the subject, a view shared by many parents.

According to the children, the teacher said that it would be all right for them to go to the class without telling their parents. I don't know if this was an accurate account of the incident, but the children did not return to public school. As I remember, they had work sent home at first, then Frank decided he wanted them to join with another family homeschool. Several families in the group held their own homeschools. Some of them joined together for a more rounded experience.

There are many successful homeschools across the country, producing well-educated well-adjusted young adults. Our experience was not as positive. Frank had a habit of telling us what he wanted us to do, without providing the tools necessary to do the job. Paula was given the daunting task of organizing and teaching us homeschool with the assistance of some of Helen's older girls, who were only fifteen and thirteen. Had it been me trying to teach, I think my head would have spun around, then exploded.

I can still see it in my mind, the West Temple house, upstairs with a long rectangular table and the children seated around. Helen had no workbooks or readers to work with, only surplus computer paper, the folded perforated sheets and pencils. So many children on different levels, it must have been challenging for her, to say the least. Still, she put her all into that impossible task.

The subject of our children's education spans many years, involving different people, places and homes. This Order evolved over a period of time.

For a time, most of our children attended the group private school while we lived at the "Pink house." This is when the Order purchased a bus and everyone rode together. I helped from time to time with a pre-school for some of the smaller children for a couple of hours on my days off.

Once the move was made from the pink house to the Butterfield Canyon property, which I will tell you about later, a homeschool was organized for all the children living there. I am sure the women gave it their best, but it was awful. I was already pulling away from Frank with his demands and had enough of the homeschool. I had been married twelve years by this time trying to make this work.

As the new school year approached, I decided that I was sending my children to the private school which was run by the group and told Frank that I needed a car to get us there. I got his look that could freeze water, but I was past caring. The afternoon before school started, I was given an unregistered, uninsured, dilapidated car, but I didn't care—it had wheels.

Undaunted, I set out for school and got a ticket for not being registered, which I gave to Frank. School was about ten miles away, but eventually I was moved to a trailer home across the street. This made things much easier as we could walk to school.

Unfortunately, it also made it easy for my youngest boy to leave kindergarten when he felt he was done. The teachers would come looking for me, saying that they couldn't find him. I would go over to the trailer and there he would be, playing in that cold home, happy as a lark.

Tuition for this private school was paid for by my teaching a few lower grade classes at the amount of fifty dollars a month. Along with three days of classes came two days of homeschool. I continued to work 3-11 shifts, leaving my oldest to tend in the evening. It was not an ideal situation, but I had to juggle the best I could.

However, after a year and a half, it was clear the private school was not working. My children were falling behind. My oldest was going to night school to graduate high school. Summoning my courage, I told Frank that I was sending my oldest son, who was thirteen, to public school.

It was all I could do not to throw up as I said the words, then waited for a response. It was the middle of the school year, but I knew my boy was floundering and needed help. If I had asked, Frank would have said "no" and put my son in the care of a more "faithful" wife, probably at the yellow house, the home that Grace and Betty lived in.

But my mind was made up and I asked Frank if he would give our son a father's blessing to help him with the transition. Frank refused and would not give one, saying that he would not bless something he didn't agree with.

Thankfully, my son didn't know about it at the time, as it would have crushed him. I prayed over him as he slept that night. I think God hears a mother's prayer.

By the next school year, all my children were in public school, receiving the help they needed. One of my daughters learned to read watching *Sesame Street*. The other, it turned out, was dyslexic. This would have never been discovered if their father had had his way.

18

JENNY

———◦•◦———

BABY JENNY WAS HELEN'S seventh child and wasn't thriving. She seemed to have one setback after another and through a chain of events, was admitted to Primary Children's Hospital. Somehow, Nelly became aware that the medical staff concluded Jenny had been neglected and suspected child abuse. According to Nelly, Jenny was to be placed into foster care.

That night, Frank and another man went to the hospital, finding Jenny dressed and ready to be picked up. Frank took the baby and hurried toward an exit as the other man took off in the opposite direction with an empty blanket in his hands. Meeting up outside, they disappeared into the night

This put the family into flight, scattering in different directions. At first, I didn't know what had happened, only that I was to go to another location and wait to hear from my husband. Helen must have been terrified as she scrambled to pack up her children and escape the nightmare of a possible investigation, still not knowing where her baby was.

Within a few days, I found that Helen and Paula were hiding in southern Utah in a remote place under appalling conditions. They were living in an abandoned barn. There were spaces between the weathered boards of the walls and no windows. There was little ventilation to relieve the stifling heat and they were plagued with flies in stunning number. They had an outhouse but no facility to bathe or do laundry. Water was hauled from a well nearby.

Nelly and I stayed in town to work, but Frank never returned to his previous employment. He was afraid he would be found and subsequently, Jenny would be taken from us. Nelly and I moved from one friend's home to another in case we were followed. I went to work with a twenty-dollar bill pinned to my underwear in case I did not have time to collect my handbag before I had to run away.

I drove with Frank to see the family one time and could hardly believe my eyes. I had never seen such awful conditions. Yet there were those women, trying to hold things together. Some children playing outside had decided to see what was inside an apricot pit. After they struck it with a hammer many times, the seed was broken free. Thinking that it was a nut, one of Helen's little girls ate some of them and became terribly ill.

I had no idea, but apricot pits contain amygdalin which is a poisonous compound. Eaten in a large number they can be very dangerous. She had some short-term effects which included difficulty formulating sentences, processing what was said to her and a slightly stumbling, awkward gait. Over time, she fully recovered, becoming a mother herself. One would never know that she came so close to death.

Because of such close scrutiny of Helen and her children, Frank was given the use of a trailer home on the Pinesdale, Montana ranch. She was out of sight in some ways and definitely out of mind for Frank. Once again, she was at the mercy of some of the kind folks who lived up there. She and Nelly had lived there as children, so it must have been more comfortable to be around people Helen knew. Frank would make the trip once a month or so, with token offerings of food and other needful things. He would arrive Saturday evening and leave Sunday afternoon. Frank had found another corner to shove this sweet wife into, expecting other men to provide care and protection.

19

THE BOOKSTORE ERA

FRANK HAD LOST HIS job when he disappeared with Jenny from the hospital. I was going to say that we were in a bad way financially, but it seems redundant as we have always been that way and continued to be until after I left. I suppose Frank was afraid to apply for jobs for fear of being confronted by the police or social services. That was 1970-71 and aside from an odd job occasionally, he was never gainfully employed again.

Eventually, the family returned to the Salt Lake area. What a sight they were! Helen and Paula were bone weary from their experience, the children bedraggled. They looked like refugees. Page was still showing the effects of arsenic poisoning. We all returned to the Sandy home, but under a lot of secrecy. We began to use the double wide garage in Granger to relieve the overflow, once Nelly decided to rejoin us.

Some men in the group decided that a business was the way to go for Frank and since he was the studious type, decided that a book store would be ideal, so they funded the project. Unfortunately, this was not a good idea for several reasons. First, Frank was not business minded, and he made some irreparable mistakes early on that made success nearly impossible. Second, it was difficult to succeed when there were already several well-established bookstores in town, as well as a few other minor specialty stores.

Business was poor from the beginning, with only people in the "group" buying from him. They purchased mostly LDS books from local publishers, one or two books at a time, keeping the profit margin very low. Frank responded by increasing his prices. Soon people caught on and eventually stopped buying from him at all.

Because Frank was a member of the council, people would come into the store to speak with him. Some had doctrinal questions. Others were investigating the group. Yet others came for personal guidance.

For the most part, I was at the front of the store in case someone came in. I also answered the phone and took messages for Frank as he was not to be disturbed until afternoon when we had prayers. I had a brand-new baby at the time, which made it especially difficult to be in a store with no crib or place to care for him.

To try to make it work, the store location was moved twice in the downtown area. Each had a retail store front and a large back room with an upstairs area where Frank had his office and books. With the opportunity to isolate himself from all else, he spent countless hours reading and preparing for his cottage meetings.

From my perspective, the bookstore only allowed Frank to further insulate himself from others, including his family. At the first location, I was a new mom trying to care for my baby and work in the store. I couldn't seem to do both. It was so frustrating. Then I was criticized, as well, since I could not seem to do a good enough job to please my husband. I felt trapped in that cavernous vault as time passed painfully and slowly. It was especially hard when the time came that I had to leave my baby at home to be cared for. The store location was moved to a suburb where the rent was less, but the business continued to fail, the leader of the group saw what was happening and told Frank that he should close the store and get another job. Frank had been encouraged to do this for almost two years but would not hear of it. He made it a matter of principal saying that God didn't give up on us and he was not going to give up on the bookstore. This was just another excuse to refuse direction from someone in authority. That type of rhetoric was typical of the way Frank conducted his family, the Order, and his life in general. Everything was on his terms, and he used anything that would let him do as he pleased.

It is human nature to want what we can't or don't have. I was the logical one to work at the bookstore as Helen needed to be at home with the children, along with Paula, who was still in hiding. Nelly worked full time at the hospital. Once my baby was old enough to stay home, I would go to the store in the morning and then work the 3-11 shift at the hospital. There were feelings that I was lucky to be at the store, but I would have gladly changed places. They were awfully long days as Frank wanted to leave right after six a.m. prayers. The family gathered for prayer at six a.m. and six p.m., so that meant a long twelve-hour day for me.

He went back to the store until he had to leave in the evening to arrive home in time for the Perry Mason T.V. show, which was 10:30 p.m. Once Frank established something, it became a routine and never changed. He stuck to that time frame until I left him.

The wives at home were expected to stay up until he arrived and wait until he was done watching the program. To go to bed before that was an affront to him, even if you were dead tired. When ready, he would get out his notebook and leaf through it. He would say the name of the wife he would sleep with, whereupon she would get up and follow him to the bedroom. All of this happened early on in my marriage. It was degrading. It felt as if I was in a harem, just a number, removing all sense of value.

At prayer times, when Frank was home, we always knelt for prayer. After the prayer was said, Frank would stand, then extend his hand to the first wife for her to get up, then the second and so on until all the wives were standing. Then he would say to the children, "You may rise." No one was to get off their knees until he said those words. He exerted such a powerful psychological influence, couched control in a religious frame and placed himself as if he was next to the God we had just prayed to.

Retrospect can be alarming. Thinking about it now, our passive behavior back then stuns me. We were sitting around at his feet, catering to him as if we were his pets and doing anything we could to please him.

During the bookstore era, a single man named Garrett came into the group who was drawn to Frank and our family. He was a decent fellow who seemed to need a place to belong. Unfortunately for him, it was us. He soon began to look on Frank as a father figure and called him that.

Garrett lived in the back of the bookstore in two of the locations. He gave his paycheck to Frank to help the family, receiving only a little money in return for bus fare to and from work. Those were sparse conditions. He had a cot to sleep on, nowhere to bathe and only a sink and toilet that went with it. He also had a small fridge and a hot plate to fix meals with food from the greens. The mothers did his laundry.

I don't know what engendered such devotion, but he stayed with us for several years. He had two children, Tracy, age twelve, and John, age eight, who lived with grandparents out of state. Garrett wanted to have them move in with us as he missed them very much. But as with all else, Frank was the one to make the plan to get the children back, which included a fake marriage between Garrett and myself.

Why the children couldn't just come to live with their dad, I do not know. But, the deception turned out badly. We were trying to live a lie. We never slept in the same room, let alone the same bed. More than once, one or the other of Garrett's children came into my room and found Frank was in my bed. The whole affair was devastating to them. This was not a new happy home, but a messy, crowded, confusing life. It was so contrary to the type of life they had lived with their grandparents.

Within six months, Tracy and John had found a way to be rescued from the terrible situation. Tracy became friendly with a couple who attended the group church meetings. Tracy was so unhappy and explained the situation she and her brother were in. Rather than contact authorities, the couple took Tracy and John in. What a tragedy all this was as it created such a barrier between the children and their dad. It ended up wounding them deeply.

Frank's way of thinking was so different to pretty much everyone else, yet we fell in line with the assumption that he knew much more than we did. We thought that we didn't see the whole picture. Sadly, the picture he offered us was badly distorted, and we lacked the courage to speak up and demand better.

20

ONE HOUSE, TWO HOUSE, THREE HOUSE MORE ...

———◦•◦•◦———

OUR POLYGAMOUS FAMILY NEVER owned a home. We moved frequently. Much like the illustrations in Dr. Seuss books, the homes we lived in were often ramshackle and always bursting at the seams.

My experience began with a modest bungalow style home in Sandy, where I first met the family. Every inch of space was utilized. There were three bedrooms upstairs, one for Nelly when she stayed there, one for Helen and the other four children. Two bedrooms downstairs were unfinished. Paula's bedroom had a small window and just enough room for a bed, dresser and crib, while mine was even smaller with no window and just enough room for a fold-up bed and dresser. Whenever Nelly felt like spending time there, it was standing room only with enough chaos to make the paint peel off the walls. One little bathroom served the whole household!

Keeping us company in the basement, was a storage room and Frank's library, both of which were always locked. The rest of the space was for laundry with an old-style Dexter washing machine and a sink in which to rinse the laundry. The kitchen was big enough for the demands placed on it, including a perpetual stack of dishes to be washed. Off the kitchen was a small eating area that blended into the living room. Well-worn couches against the walls and the big "father's" chair in a corner rounded out the ensemble.

One part of the family or another was always on the move, shuffled around to suit some unknown criteria, at least unknown to everyone but our husband. I think it was Frank's way of ensuring that we interacted with each other on his terms.

Wives learned to get along with each other as well as the children. Most of this time, Nelly lived in what we called the Granger home, which was not a house, but a double garage made from what looked like railroad ties. There was a small kitchen with a wall strip heater for winter warmth, a tiny bathroom with just enough room for a toilet, shower and sink. Then there was a small bedroom off the kitchen while the rest of the space was an open living room and bedroom in one. The redeeming feature was an enormous backyard where the children had more freedom to play than ever before. There were two huge apricot trees with a garden space. Once the apricots ripened, we would beg people to come and pick all they wanted. Still, I can't tell you how many bottles of apricots we put up. This was when I learned how to bottle food—it was not my favorite thing to do. Our sweet Helen would insist on bottling zucchini, which, if you don't know, turns to mush, but we could not dissuade her from it.

Frank had a divided family on his hands. Nelly living in the Granger home and the rest of us in the Sandy home. This allowed Nelly to remain isolated from the rest of the family. She was receiving food stamps while we were still relying on greens. No one knew about this until much later when it finally came out, that and sub for Santa gifts at Christmas time. Frank did not allow us to celebrate Christmas or Easter, as it was a Pagan holiday, he said.

Harry Neilson and his family lived in the home situated closer to the road than the garage I mentioned. One night the home caught fire and burned to the ground. Tragically, three of their little boys died of smoke inhalation and were found huddled together in the bathroom. Insurance paid for the building of a new home, but the Neilson family only lived there for a short while. They moved to another state; I am not sure why.

While Nelly was in the process of moving, her children would stay with us in the new home. When Nelly's son Zachary, was blessed as a baby, Frank said among other things, that the child would be misunderstood throughout his life. Some mothers do not readily accept that their little ones can get into mischief or not mind their parents. Whenever one of the mothers brought something to Nelly's attention about Zachary misbehaving, she would go back to that baby blessing. We must not know what really happened, someone was not telling the truth, he was being misunderstood. It didn't take many years for Zachary to catch on.

Zachary was seven or eight at this time, and as I looked out of the kitchen window, I saw him climbing into the dumpster of a business next door. I suppose we had set an example when dumpster diving for food. He wanted to see if there was anything useful in that dumpster but had been told to stay out of it. I called out his name telling him to get out of the bin, he looked up, jumped on his bike and rode off. A small thing really, but it had become an issue, so I brought it up to his mom telling her what happened. This was risky business as Nelly and I did not get along. Nelly went to Frank saying that Zachary denied this. Next thing, Frank and Nelly came to me saying that I must be wrong, it must have been some other child. I repeated my experience, to no avail. Their denial was relentless. All I had wanted was to let Nelly know what had happened and leave it alone. Disgusted, I said that I supposed that it was in the realm of worldly possibility that there could have been somewhere, somehow a boy who resembled Zachary. That that child had blond hair and a striped tee shirt just like his who looked at me when I called his name. That was it! That was the answer they concluded. The boy was being misunderstood. It didn't take long for him to learn that being misunderstood could get him out of a lot of trouble.

This paved the way for further, more frequent misbehavior. Zachary would not behave when being tended by his older sister. He assaulted one of Helen's daughters who was babysitting Nelly's children while she was at work. As this girl was calling one of the other mothers for help, he grabbed the receiver from her hand and struck her with it. Finally, Frank sent Grace to live with Nelly to tend. Grace was continually disrespected and was nothing more than a servant. Still, there were no repercussions, he just got away with increasingly worse behavior.

While living at the pink house, Zachary was seen coming out of an apartment of one of the families living there. Money and a few items were reported missing from the same people in the same time frame. Two little girls from another family told their parents that Zachary had been touching them where he shouldn't. Things went missing at the yellow house when he was the only one who could have or would have taken them. Finally, Frank was forced to confront this now fourteen-year-old. All Zachary had to do was to say, "No, father, I didn't do it," and that was that. The family of the little girls left the Order, as we would come to call the people we closely associated with, to protect them.

These were sorrowful times and events, as this boy was out of control with no one to reign him in. He was sent to the yellow house to live with Frank which was a sore trial for those women. They had to deal with him while Frank spent his time in his office.

Over the years, I have wondered if Zachary's life would have been different if I had not given in to Frank and Nelly. Probably not, but I can't help but wonder. The larger problem was, so many children to be watched over by one mom or an older child and a father who took no responsibility for them. Every child gets into some mischief and

Zachary's was by far the worst outcome. So easy for kids to fall through the cracks. Zachary was by far the most damaging experience.

SHORTLY AFTER THAT, FRANK rented the new home and Helen, Paula and I moved into it. It was new, clean and we could spread out! We still had our old worn out furniture, but it was wonderful, considering what we left behind. Along with our furniture was "father's chair," the dilapidated overstuffed chair that was designated for Frank's use only. It was a "felony" for anyone to sit in it. I remember chastising many a child for sitting in that stupid chair.

After about a year, the house was sold, and we were looking for somewhere new to live. Frank rented out the Sandy home in case we needed to come back to it.

The next place was an old, fairly run down home on West Temple Street, which had an eerie feeling to it, especially upstairs. It had a back porch which led into the kitchen, very small with a minute pantry and as we found out later, cockroaches. Holes in the linoleum rounded out the overall effect. There was a large, at least to us, dining room with a built-in sideboard typical of the early 1900's. The adjoining living room was separated from the dining room by tall, double pocket doors. This room had a large window which had the top one-third part of the glass etched, causing the sunlight to break into prism colors, sending them dancing across the living room. What a delight in a most mundane life.

The hardwood floors in those rooms were so well worn that the surface reminded me of my grandmother's wooden kitchen table. Its surface was worn by frequent scrubbing with a bar of sand soap, a sturdy brush and a copious application of elbow grease. We had two bedrooms and the bathroom downstairs, with my room upstairs. My children slept on bunk beds in the hallway.

It was not unusual to have all of the children at our house after school, upwards of fifteen. I was the mother at home during the day and had spent hours cleaning prior to their arrival, which meant that there was at least a little peace and quiet. As I sat in that blissful silence, from the distance came the rumbling of children home from school, like the thunder of a heard of buffalo. The sound grew louder until it burst through the door, children shedding coats and dropping their backpacks when something snapped inside of me.

"Oh, no you don't," I called out. "Don't you dare drop your stuff in here! Take it to your rooms right now!" Somewhat surprised, they stopped in their tracks, slowly picked their things up and began to move towards their rooms. Noise burst forth again, but I had defended my prize cleanliness, secured it for however brief a time, and it was mine.

It was like herding cats most of the time, so many children and still the numbers grew. This home is where I finally got over the chicken pox and gave birth to my third child. This was 1975. By this time, I was drowning emotionally and was for the first time thinking about leaving.

Coming home from work one evening, I saw Frank's silhouette through the dining room window as I walked along the driveway. For the first time in my marriage, I felt a moment of fear, the kind I had with my dad. I realized that I was trapped! I had children but couldn't prove they were mine and had no money to make an escape. I managed to shove those thoughts down somewhere inside of me, along with all the other emotions I was trying to pretend didn't exist; somehow, I would survive.

It seemed that we mothers were always overwhelmed, with never enough of what we needed to care for our children. One mother stayed home to care for the children of those of us who worked many hours at low paying jobs, signing our paychecks over to Frank but seeing no result for our labor.

One of the worst and most far reaching things happened while living in this home. The washing machine had been broken for over a week and the laundry was gaining on us. I got some money from Frank to do a few loads at the laundromat. Diapers were a priority, I could hang them to dry at home along with as many clothes as I could get washed.

That day, I piled the children into the station wagon to play at the park, leaving the older girls to watch over them while I took clothes to the laundromat. Loading the machines, I returned to the park and realized that a child was missing. She must have fallen asleep somewhere in the house. I was in a hurry and didn't count heads, at least not accurately. Rushing home, I was greeted by a police officer sitting in the kitchen with the child on his lap.

I felt awful on many levels. First, I had left this little girl asleep and hadn't even noticed. Second, we had just gotten "greens" and they were sitting in the boxes on the back porch, some in the kitchen and it looked like the garbage that it was. Not only did his report state that there was "rotten food" in the house, but gaping holes in the floor, which would have been the linoleum.

Worst of all, it turned out that a neighbor had found her walking down the street crying and called the police. I think I would have done the same thing if I found a child alone in those circumstances. My negligence and being in such a hurry caused us a lot of trouble, it is a wonder that the state didn't take away all the children. It caused a lot of problems for our family, not only because of the living conditions, but because ours was a plural family.

Not too surprisingly, we moved rather quickly from the home on West Temple Street. Frank's solution was to run and hide rather than clear up our problems. We moved to a home that one of the men in the Order had found for rent. He would be paying the rent and utilities and he and his family would live there with me, Paula and our children. Helen was sent to live with another family in the Order. This was not especially unusual.

During this time, Frank still spent most of his time at the bookstore, holding meetings and moving from house to house, spending the night with a wife. There was little income and we were being supported by other men by providing housing for us.

Considering the numbers, we had to fit into pretty much any home, the houses all seemed small and inade-quate. In this one, the plumbing was faulty, but at least we had two working toilets!

The house was not without its charm, though, as it was

another early twentieth century home. Light switches were the kind you twist rather than flip on. Part of a damaged wall revealed its old lath and plaster walls, with the slats of wood positioned very closely together and secured to a stud. The lime-based mortar, which was often reinforced with horse hair, filled the small spaces between each lath. Finished with a coat of finishing plaster, the walls were covered with wallpaper or paint. These details stuck in my mind because I love old homes, especially when they are kept in their period.

My room was upstairs, which I liked as it gave me some privacy. Not peace and quiet however; there was a cubby across the hall that the children loved to play in. My room had a small window. The window proved to be too tempting for curious children wishing to climb out onto the roof, which came to a screaming halt! No more children climbing onto the roof!

Regardless of the home's shortcomings, this was the summer of my content. Paula and I seemed to work together fairly effortlessly.

The household chores she didn't like, I didn't mind and vice versa. We took turns cooking, while I still went for greens. We tended each other's children, taking turns when one of us worked at our jobs, so there was a sense of being comfortable with our situation. Children still didn't want their mom to go to work, but feelings were not so intense.

One day, though, my little girl decided to fool me by hiding in the back of one of the cars parked in the backyard. Her plan was to stay hidden until I was on the way to work, then jump up to reveal herself, expecting that I would have to take her home and would not be able to work that evening. But she got into the wrong car, sweet girl. She was found hours later sleeping on the backseat, clutching my faded old—used to be hot pink—night gown. It could have worked!

This house became known as the "Red house," since it was situated on a street named Redwood Road, following Frank's penchant for code and secrecy. The canal ran past the house. Before I knew that the water was not the cleanest, I would turn the water onto the front lawn, not caring that we didn't have a lawnmower. At least the grass lived. The kids and I would slide around on the grass, becoming soaking wet and having the time of our lives as we let off a lot of steam.

Showers and clean clothes followed those moments of reckless abandon because Frank insisted that the children be kept indoors, with little exception. So, it was a risky proposition playing outside like that. Had he seen us, I would have had to listen to the disobedient wife discourse along with, "How could you risk the family's safety again?"

Additionally, there was always the underlying, suffocating threat of having my children getting sent to a more "obedient" wife. In reality, he meant Nelly, who was not more obedient, though she appeared that way to him, and she disliked most of our young'uns besides. Helen couldn't take care of her own children very well, so they wouldn't go there. Frank had a very tight grip on us and we had to ask permission to go anywhere or do anything.

I had to face it, I had a very cluttered and messy bedroom! I never seemed to get around to cleaning it, as I was so busy with everything else. At least that's how it was in my mind. One day, one of the wives of a council member invited me to spend some time with her in her home for a few hours or so. It was embarrassing, but I had to ask for permission. Frank said that I had to clean my room first. I felt like I was being treated as a child, but I cleaned my room, just so I could go to visit. I know ... I know, a real head shaker!!

We were given a milk goat while living at the red house and I learned how to milk it. It was such a wonderful gift to have milk for our children. Sometimes there was enough to give them all a small glass of this blessed milk. It even tasted good, not at all as strong as goat milk can be.

Milking was at times disastrous as the goat would be fussy and knock the bucket over. With a whack on the rump, she would turn her head as if to say, "What?" We fed her leftover produce and Paula's dad built her a shelter. As winter came, with my being a city girl, I decided the goat needed a blanket. Lesson learned! She just shook it off.

The boxes from getting greens would accumulate over a few weeks, so one evening, Paula and I decided to burn them. Next thing we knew, we heard sirens and then the fire department pulled up. The neighbor thought our house was on fire. We did not know that it was illegal to burn things in the yard inside the city limits, but we did have a hose in our hands in case the fire spread. We were lucky not to get a citation.

While in this home, another wife joined the family. What a lovely woman she was, so happy to be one of us. The evening she was to be married, we purchased a bouquet for her and left it sitting in water just inside the back door. Somehow, the goat got loose and bumped the backdoor open and chomped off the tops of all the flowers, leaving only stems. We stood there in the doorway, trying not to laugh. It looked like a scene from a comedy show. We were somewhere between laughing and crying, hoping we hadn't jinxed her.

The land that the red house sat on, as well as much of the vacant surrounding land, became zoned for commercial use. It was subsequently sold. So once again, we were looking for a home.

21

PINK HOUSE

———◦•◦———

THE "PINK HOUSE" WAS a home in south Sandy that was huge by our standards which had come to Frank's attention. The owner wanted to sell at the time, but it had proven difficult, so he agreed to rent it to the Order.

I could see why it was hard to sell. The structure was a monstrosity, sitting on almost an acre of sage brush and dirt. The property finally did sell to some real estate investors upon which Frank pronounced the transaction an assault on "God's work." It was just people conducting business. But before that, we were able to rent there for several years.

The pink house was named for the pink-colored brick it was made of. It really had to be seen to be appreciated. The house was a sprawling metropolis which was the official starting place of Frank's "united effort." Everyone involved called it the "Order" and the name stuck. He had a strong following of men who saw this as the next step in their spiritual growth. Intended to become a center of communal living, it started out with clearly defined living quarters, which soon filled to over-capacity. "United" implies an all-for-one and one-for-all venture. But, as with any financial endeavor involving our family, with Frank still unemployed and all of us living on one Nurse's Aide income, we never paid our fair share.

To give an idea of the layout, there was the original single-family dwelling with a basement apartment. The owner had built a two-story addition which was larger than the original home, forming an L shape.

Separate from all of this was a large metal shed, uninsulated but with two tiny windows. It was sweltering hot in the summer and equally cold in the winter, without running water or sewage connections. This would become living quarters for Helen and her children. Frank framed in some rooms in the shed for Helen and sheets were hung from them to provide a degree of privacy.

In all, some seventy men, women and children lived in the complex. Two men and their families occupied the upstairs, sharing the kitchen and living room. Paula and I lived in the basement apartment with our nine children. It also served Helen's family for kitchen and bathroom. This brought the number of occupants in the basement to around eighteen. Two large families occupied the addition or wing, as we often called it, without hurting each other or coming to blows. At some point, the men added an entrance doorway on one side of the main floor level of the addition. It was not a good idea because, when it rained, water gushed down the hill, through a space under the door, into the bottom floor corridor and out another doorway.

Before long, the men decided that we needed more bedroom space for the children and turned the garage into a bedroom with several sets of bunks. There was no heat or ventilation, and for a while, two of my girls slept there. My two boys slept on a single bed in the space that held the furnace and led to the upstairs. It made me nervous when the furnace kicked on because it ferociously sent out a lot of heat into that space.

At some point, the basement wall leading to the wing was broken through for easy access to the addition from our basement. That space was where a washer and occasionally working dryer were placed. We had a light bulb hanging from a wire, so we could see what we were doing. It was also the first place anyone would look for a light bulb if they were out. Out of patience with pilfered light bulbs, Paula put a sign by it which said, "Don't even think about it."

With a new family moving into the pink house, another apartment was built, including a kitchen and bathroom above the garage. All the extra building that was done was accomplished without the benefit of a building permit or safety inspections. Frank felt that it was nobody's business.

Helen was moved into the shed which consisted only of the framing and corrugated metal sheets. Come winter, a wood burning stove was installed in the shed for warmth. Somehow a fire started, I think the door of the stove was left open and sparks spread, so did the fire. Now Helen needed somewhere to live, besides the basement.

The men commenced building another floor over the

wing, making three stories in all. It was framed in with a plywood roof, minus tar paper. The outside walls had window spaces cut out. The rooms were divided by hanging sheets from two by fours and sheets over the windows. There was little protection from the elements and they had to take refuge in our basement at one point, when the electricity in our kitchen went out. We checked the light bulb and the breaker to no avail. Finally, we strung an extension cord from my room to a lamp, so we could get by.

Later, Frank had a man in the Order, who was an electrician by trade, check out the wiring. After removing some ceiling tiles, he said that whoever wired the basement must have been paid by the splice. With trepidation, I looked at Paula and said, "For the rest of our natural lives." Whereupon, she nodded in agreement. It sounds like a sentence of some kind and in a way, it was, as not much was repaired. We just learned to get by.

During this same time, Frank's stress level must have been rising. We asked him for money to purchase something we needed. I don't remember what it was, but it didn't sit well with him.

In frustration he said, "Well, I'll just have to get a job."

This was music to our ears. *Well, all right*, I thought! The next day, while at work, I looked at the employment ads in the newspaper. Low and behold, there it was, a job for a technical writer! With much anticipation I cut it out, saving it for the next time I saw him.

He was not as impressed as I was but couldn't say a word against me. He didn't do anything about it getting the job, either.

I can only imagine that Frank's thought upon seeing the pink house was that there were so many possibilities to add onto what was already there. He liked to build things, and nothing was finished here. There was no sheetrock, insulation or paint. Without thought as to the temporary nature of a rental, he poured a great deal of material and countless man hours into this house. Yet, it was something we would, at some time, have to walk away from.

The work project on this rental was in effect for several years and became mandatory for all the men in the Order. There would be no exception. If a man did not show up to work on the project, he was severely reprimanded. It was risky behavior on Frank's part, considering how much he needed those men to fill his financial needs, as well as his need to have a loyal following. As with many facets of life with Frank, once something began, it never ended, never changed, even if change was needed. Instead of working on the house being a bonding experience between Frank and his sons, it became an oppressive requirement. He was not accustomed to being around the children. He was short of patience, not knowing how to direct them and not realizing their abilities or limitations.

The one bright spot for the boys was when some of the other men brought their sons to work with them. I imagine it was Frank's intent to teach our sons how to work and be reliable. But how could a child learn that from a man who had been unemployed for years and a once-a-week effort is all they saw?

One winter's day, I watched Frank, Betty, and another man, along with a couple of boys, trudge out into a snowy field with their heads down. They were silent and cold. What a forlorn sight they were. They were to cut down some trees for Helen's wood burning stove. The trees were only dormant and would not burn well, if at all. It was so typical of our lives. The need for wood had existed for several months. But not until the need was imminent did Frank do anything about it. How could children learn to be strong providers with such a poor and conflicting example?

As the pink house population grew, so did Frank's propensity for doing almost everything en-masse. For about a minute, we had family night on Sundays after church. But that quickly changed since we were no longer a family, but an extended family. As a result, our "family night" was attended by Order families and was open to anyone who wished to come. It became a side show!

All the school age children at the pink house attended the group's private school. So, I suppose that it was an economically sound idea to buy a bus. The first was a small blue bus that probably held a third of the number of people a regular school bus would hold. Jason, an Order member, drove it to school three times a week as we had homeschool two days.

Preventative maintenance was never at the top of the list for our own vehicles, and that included the bus. It is little wonder that the blue bus didn't last long. Next was a full-sized yellow school bus that Frank loved to drive. But he drove it without a CDL (commercial driver's license). For some reason, Frank always thought that secular laws did not apply to him. We would arrive in the bus to church, or at a park, whereupon we would swarm out, often to people's amusement and sometimes to their disdain. But we never went unnoticed.

One evening, while Frank was negotiating some gears in the bus on a hill, we began to roll backwards, which made us all uneasy. The Jordan River flows through the Salt Lake Valley and happened to be just over a small hill from where we were. When someone began singing "Jordan River, Here We Come" to the tune of "California, Here We Come," the comical effort was not wasted, and we broke out laughing.

Our bus took a school trip all the way to the Midwest, only breaking down twice. There was a second yellow school bus which filled the previous transportation needs, but this one took a load of adults and children to a small township in Montana. Grace was having heart problems but insisted on going, to be obedient to her husband. The problem was that she spent most of her time on a makeshift bed at the back of the bus. Before the first hundred miles, I think most of us wished we could turn back as the seats were hard and taking a nap was impossible. Crying babies and energy-filled toddlers added to the chaos.

Fortunately, for the next trip, I was helping Francine with a delivery and was therefore able to keep my children at home with me. What a blissful time it was, everyone gone and just my children and me rattling around in the house.

In September of 1978, we took another trip, this time to southern Utah. Frank was the council representative to a small group of plural families living in a community near Motoqua. In the 1970's, two brothers were sent, with their families to establish residence. Others of the group joined them over time to develop the location into a successful venture. This was part of the D.I. ranch of Moe Dalitz/ Virginia Hill fame. Rancho was part of the D.I. ranch, a subsidiary of Unified Industries and of Apostolic United Brethren. This was all tied in with the acquisition of the ranch and Hill's money. That however, is another story.

The bus was crammed with Frank's Order members along with their children and our family. The trip was a welcome break for me and my three children from the routine of our lives. The two-hour drive passed quickly as we enjoyed the scenery of southern Utah. Once at our destination, the children poured out of the bus onto the expanse of grass and pasture land. I loved watching my little ones run and play in the fresh air and sunshine. There was an enormous weeping willow tree with massive branches supporting several rope and tire swings, which proved impossible for the kids to ignore. A small stream flowed through part of the property and my boys caught a trout in their hands. Such squeals of delight gave me a deep sense of peace and gratitude for the experience of being their mom. There was not space for all to sleep in the homes and some of us slept outdoors with the mosquitoes.

Frank held his meetings to which attendance was mandatory, but there was an overall lightness to the mood of the weekend. Around five o'clock on Sunday, our host families began to make macaroni and cheese for the lot of us. It takes a while to whip up mac and cheese for that many people. Frank became unreasonably anxious and insisted on leaving. He would not wait for the meal, leaving them with huge pots of food and a bus load of hungry people, especially children.

People clamored for Frank's discourses, hanging on every word. Consequently, he relinquished one of his favorite things, driving the bus. One of the men took over as driver and Frank began preaching. Listening was difficult as the children were hungry and tired.

People in the first three rows could hear him but the rest could not. To remedy this, Frank had two people to act as verbal "runners." He would say a few sentences then wait for the men to relay his words. It seemed very odd to me, and it continued for an hour or more. These idiosyncrasies proved to be an embarrassment to the wives, but Frank loved the limelight. He was in rebellion toward the other men on the council who looked down on him and did so by demanding a following of devoted individuals. My own opinion is that Dr. Allred lent credibility to Frank but after he was killed, Frank was at odds with other council members.

Finally, that bus broke down and was parked at the Butterfield Canyon property until the county towed both it and another truck away. The land was cleared of all the buildings to make way for a wild horse sanctuary. I will be sharing more about that place.

While living in the pink house, I would go for greens weekly. We had to use the vehicle of someone in the complex as we did not have a car and Frank would not allow us to take his. Once home with boxes of produce, breadstuffs and whatever dairy I might find, we unloaded. The food was set out for everyone there to come and take what they wanted. We lived off the rest. I grew to resent this because the other families could purchase what else they needed. Word of my feelings got to one of the men in the complex and he brought me a small package of puffed wheat. I don't know what he meant by it. It embarrassed me, and I was angry at the same time.

Now those times sound so petty to me and I am ashamed of my feelings, but we went without for such a long time that it was easy to lose perspective. Those husbands not only paid Order dues to Frank but paid the rent and utilities. The electric bill alone must have been astronomical with all those people living there.

On one of the greens days, Frank did not endear himself to me. While carrying boxes of produce into the house, he stood there watching me going back and forth.

He made the comment, "Women were built for carrying heavy things because they carry and deliver babies. Men," he continued, "don't have those types of muscles."

That statement whizzed right past me. Maybe I was tired; maybe I was past caring; perhaps it just didn't register. To me it was some lame reasoning; justifying his lazy worthless self. It was the reaffirmation that he was above such menial labor. It was women's work! I kept moving along, doing that which I was supposed to do.

Then it registered, words from years ago that, "Women work as does the rest of the body. The man is the head and has the intellect." *What*, I thought, *are we nothing more to him than possessions to do his bidding?* Stunned by the realization but unable to speak, I just kept moving. I was fast losing what respect there was left toward him. He had very subtly referred to the family being the man's possession, it was part of the continuing rhetoric. Now I was wondering if he thought of us as pots and pans, or maybe a work horse.

Typically, Frank would give us twenty dollars about every three or four weeks for our three families living at the pink house to pay for our household needs. That would include laundry soap, dish soap, toilet paper, feminine products, and bleach. Sadly, it also included groceries.

During this time, one of our mothers was expecting and nearing her due date. She needed birthing supplies; items for her new baby. She needed cloth diapers, plastic pants, diaper pins and the like. She was the senior wife and Frank gave her the money and she decided to keep it for the baby's needs, unbeknownst to the rest of us.

I kept wondering why he was not giving us anything at all. We were desperate for the most basic of necessities. Yet, he felt justified in spending $100 on a spirit level and $30 on a plumb bob, essential to continue building.

Our lives were like that for as long as I can remember. There was always a sense of hopelessness. As years passed, and our plight continued, I could not understand how Frank could be so disconnected from what was right in front of him. He distanced himself from our struggles. Staying with his books until late in the evening and leaving early in the morning must have made it easier, along with the fact that each of the mothers so readily assumed the task of making his desires come to pass.

My journal entry from Wednesday, 26 August 1981:

Morale is pretty low as we are all stretched to our

limits. Appliances break down and it takes months to get replacements and we are forced to ask other families in the house to use their appliances, no money for food or gas to put in the cars we borrow mostly for greens. Went for greens this morning praying that I would find what we needed. After several stops, I had so much food I had to leave some behind. Got good fruit; three boxes of bananas, two boxes of apples, oranges and some peaches. Three boxes of cantaloupe, two boxes of lettuce, a box of apple butter, a sack of rolls, some hot dog buns and a few sweet rolls. Also, some bread and a little milk as well.

I was late getting home and as I came through the door, Paula was telling the children to be patient as there was no food in the house. I almost cried. What a heart-breaking scene, all those mouths to feed and their father nowhere in sight.

It seemed that Frank was oblivious to and had no concern for his children's well-being. We were living hand-to-mouth all the time now. No wonder we felt so helpless.

Amid all of our hard times, an idea came to Frank, seemingly out of nowhere, never before and never since. He chose one random day to recognize our collective birthdays. It was a Sunday afternoon with the family gathered in our basement family room. There was a big overstuffed "father's chair" at one end of the rectangular room. The mothers, except for Betty, had no idea what was going on. Our children were sitting on the floor in front of him. Next to the chair was a pad of paper and a container with coins in it.

There he sat, looking very pleased as he surveyed his family. With much ceremony, he unfolded his plan. Each mother would receive five cents for every year old they were, and the children would receive one penny for each year. Paula and I looked at each other with surprise, no— disbelief. Helen and Nelly looked adoringly at him while the children squealed with delight. Grace and Betty stood by his side.

All were to form a line with each mother according to seniority. Helen was first and so on, with her children behind her from eldest to youngest. Ceremony on a grand scale! The children had no concept of what a penny or even a dime could buy. Reflecting on this, I am confident that these pennies were the only gifts their dad had ever given them.

Frank must have spent many hours figuring all that out as he had the exact amount of money to the last penny. I was trying not to dampen the children's excitement, but still, I could feel my head slightly shaking in disbelief. What a transparent act. I could only feel a mixture of disgust and anger. A penny or a nickel on a child's actual birthday every year might be something but not this. Was I becoming prideful? He was treating his wives as children!

Frank was to be the source of everything we received, all to be dispensed at his pleasure. It had nothing to do with birthdays; it was all about control. The more I thought about it, the more disgusted I became. I was truly resenting the fact that the wives carried such a heavy load, while Frank continued to bury himself in his miserable library.

There is one constant in polygamy: the pattern of control, manipulation and isolation. There comes a time when you don't know who you are anymore, only what you have become. Who you were is at best lost in the remnant of a dream.

I was the last of our family out of the pink house once we were evicted; only because it worked out that way. It was so quiet after all the chaos and noise. A feeling of nostalgia hung over me. As the sheds and wing were being razed, critters made their way into the house. One of these was a black widow spider, with eggs on her back. She seemed to be running for all she was worth and found a dark corner in what used to be the laundry room. I have smushed many a spider, but I couldn't find it in myself to kill her. She was a mother looking for a safe place for her babies. It seemed that I had been doing just that for many years. I suppose it was some odd sense of a mother's heart, even if it was for a spider.

So much happened at the pink house. I delivered a baby for one of the ladies there because the midwife had not arrived. I received the awful news of my son's death and reason began to "grease the chute" for me. There was enough for a miniseries!

Finally, the owner sold the home and property to a developer and we began to dismantle all the building supplies used to expand. They were all sent out to the Cedar Valley property, including the wood burning stove. Over the years, all of this must have been found by rabbit hunters and appeared abandoned as they have all disappeared.

Occasionally, I have driven past the old pink house. I hardly recognize it as it is surrounded now by lovely homes with well cared for homes with well cared for yards. Still, I can see the window of what was my bedroom where I delivered two children and received the awful news of Daniel's death. Nothing in life remains the same, even our memory fades: but the events recorded in our very being endures. We never forget the children we bear or the children we bury.

22

GRIEF

———◦•◦•◦———

THERE ARE EVENTS IN life that you simply do not
see coming and you are completely blindsided by
them. For me, July 8, 1980 was such a day.

My oldest son Daniel, who was nine years old at the
time, was looking forward to going with Nelly and her
family to the Cedar Valley property. They were to stay
for a week and, despite Nelly's harshness toward him, he
was happy to be going. Seeing him laughing as they drove
away, I didn't worry, thinking he would have great fun.

There were power lines running parallel to the property
line which were to be transitioned to the huge grey metal
towers which had been constructed next to them. When
Nelly and the others arrived, there was a crew of men laying
out cable and hoisting it up onto the towers. The foreman

spoke to Nelly, warning her that they would be employing a hydraulic winch to pull the cable into place. He told her that all his crew would be needed to manage the job just over the hill and to be sure to keep the children away from the cable.

She went into the trailer to play cards while the boys went out to play. Fairly naturally, the boys began to play on the cable as it would lift them up off the ground and then dump them back down. More and more of the cable would be wound up, when suddenly, the cable was pulled halfway up the height of the tower, with Daniel holding onto it.

The boys decided that he should hold onto the cable, then once at the top, climb down the tower. It made sense to nine and eleven-year-old boys. As Daniel hung there on the cable, I think that the wind took his breath away and he lost consciousness.

One of the boys later told me that he took a sharp breath in, his eyes closed, his hands relaxed, and he fell. He hit the ground with such impact that his body flipped completely over. He died there in Nelly's arms.

The workmen had noticed something on the cable and sent someone down to see what it was. Coming upon that dreadful scene, they called for a Life Flight helicopter, but it was too late.

My life had slipped into the mundane, always trying to catch up, never enough hours in a day, never enough sleep. I had been short with Daniel recently and was feeling that I needed to spend some time with him. Waiting for the washer to finish a cycle, I was sorting through some of his old school papers, trying to decide what to keep, and looking forward to his return.

It was six in the evening when my husband, Frank, called, asking me to get ready to go with him to a hospital. It was not unusual for us to visit the sick, so I didn't think much of it at first. But seconds before he came into the house, the thought that something was wrong with Daniel flashed through my mind. I brushed it aside until Frank took me to our bedroom and said bluntly, "Our son, Daniel, is dead."

I was stunned; the strength ran out of me and my knees buckled. For a time, I was so numb that I couldn't understand what people were saying. It was as if they were speaking a foreign language and I couldn't focus on anything I looked at.

Slowly, I began to process what was being said. "Dear God, how can this be, my sweet little boy dead?" I was no more to feel his sweet embrace, to feel his kiss on my cheek, to hear his voice or to run my fingers through his sandy-colored hair. I had been so busy, so tired and had been short with him. Had God taken him as punishment?

We drove in silence to Holy Cross Hospital where his small body had been flown. I seemed to be without emotion; it was so surreal. Frank wept, saying, "They had to take a pure innocent boy, I wasn't good enough."

A nurse showed us into a room where his lifeless body lay, silent and without color. My sweet boy, the blood that once gave him life coating his nostrils and teeth. I touched his thin chest with the palm of my hand and stroked his sweet face and brow.

I was living a parent's nightmare. I'd had the fear of death recently but thought it was for me. I had bought bikes for Daniel and his sister earlier in the summer but would not allow them to ride out of sight. Still, death came.

He had a broken neck, broken left arm and a compound fracture of his right femur, the bone still protruding through the muscle, as well as internal injuries. Touching his still body, I realized that he was no longer in it, but gone with angels. A nurse cut a lock of his hair for me to keep, then helped me to the car. Frank gathered information from Nelly and we drove home.

Nothing seemed real, yet my broken heart ached, and my empty arms yearned for him. I longed to hold him, but knew that I could not. The next morning, we told the other children that their brother had died and gone to heaven. I walked the house at night sobbing and softly calling his name. There was no sound from God, no sound from my boy; only empty silence surrounded me.

I felt happy while making Daniel's burial clothes, as if he were near. During that time, so many people came by to offer help, bringing food. Frank would come and go, making funeral arrangements and the like. My grief was palpable, but I busied myself with little things, mostly my children, trying to comfort them.

Once the autopsy was performed, his body was released to the mortuary and I was able to dress him. It was hard to leave him there. I felt as though I was abandoning him, even though I knew he wasn't there any longer.

Saturday, July 12, 1980, was the day we buried my son. I think I know what despair is, but there is no cure. We had a graveside service during which a monarch butterfly circled the flowers on the casket. Since then, I have felt an affinity to those beautiful creatures.

During this terrible time, Nelly didn't say much of anything. Not that she was sorry or to ask my forgiveness or even my understanding of her neglect. Instead, she had Frank bring me to her home, where she offered to give me one of her sons, one who was near Daniel's age. I looked at her in utter disbelief, my mouth unable to form words.

I told her that I did not want her child. Did she think she could pay me for the life of my son? How could I take her boy and raise him as my own? I would have resented him with every beat of my heart. This was something neither she nor Frank could make right.

The night following the accident, some detectives came to our home. I was upstairs with some of the people who lived at the pink house, some visitors as well as our family. The detectives asked me if a particular surname meant anything to me.

I told them that it did not, but it was my husband's name. Just as they spoke his name, I could see him coming upstairs with his foot on the top step. Upon hearing his name, Frank spun around and hurried back to the basement. He looked so foolish, I almost laughed at him. Nonetheless, I felt betrayed, being left to deal with the officers alone. Frank was more concerned about what might happen to him than he was in standing by my side when I needed him. He always put his own protection first, as we were to protect him from the law.

Throughout this experience, I have learned that no one

ever gets over the death of a child. The pain changes, but it never goes away. I found that I could carry the pain for just so long and then I had to put it down at the feet of my Savior, lest my heart break with no hope of repair. I also learned that the sense that someone is missing stays with a parent for a very long time.

Tears would flow with no apparent trigger or warning. They would hit me like a massive wall of water, taking my breath away, and flow with a torrent of emotion. I had dreams of another child being killed in some random way and would not allow any of my children to go anywhere without me. I felt as though I had nothing left in me, but I could not allow this heavy grief to rob us of our future.

There was room for little else, at times not even breath. Seeking refuge in routine, my days and weeks passed. Still clouded with the heavy sense of loss, time moved slowly, suspended between reality and the hope that somehow my boy would find his way home.

Eventually, we began to move forward. I loved my little ones so very much, but I was on auto pilot most of the time. I have a strong belief in an afterlife and that I would again hold Daniel once more in my arms. But it would not be soon enough.

Grief changes with the passage of time. The pain eases or perhaps dulls a little. The sense that someone is missing comes less often, while the sure bright hope of seeing him again remains clear in my mind.

However, even after more than thirty years, once in a while, I look in the mirror and see the sad clear eyes of someone who has lost the most precious of gifts, a child, one who has laid him in the darkness of the grave. From time to time, I visit that place knowing that he is not really there but am drawn to his side because that is the last place I left him.

23

THE "CEDAR VALLEY" PROPERTY

BEFORE BUTTERFIELD CANYON, WHEN we were still living in Salt Lake City, the group council had put money down on a piece of land in the Cedar Valley which is actually on the map and about fifty miles south west of Bluffdale Utah. Frank never gave us the details of financial or any other dealings, which makes it difficult to give any details about how this happened. After the trouble while living in the West Temple house, it was decided that Frank and his family were good candidates to establish the fact that someone was living at Cedar Valley.

According to my understanding, Frank was to develop the property as a refuge for our family and others who needed seclusion. It was to function along the lines of a "United Order." It was early summer 1976 when we, along with members of the Order were introduced to what was designed to be the rest of our lives. Filled with hope that we could turn this desolate, sage brush filled place into a Utopia, the mothers took a collective deep breath. We had hopes of being able to live our plural lives without interference from the outside world.

There was a run-down, single wide trailer home with no electricity, sewer or running water. This became home for Susan and her children. About fifty feet from the trailer, power lines ran north and south along the eastern side of the valley. You could hear the hum of the electricity flowing through them. New metal towers would soon be put into use to carry even more electricity to distant destinations.

For several months, Helen lived in Cedar Valley with her young children. She did all she could to survive while the rest of the family lived and worked in the city. She was very vulnerable out there. There was no phone or car in case of emergencies, and she had only the water and food brought from town.

Frequently, rabbit hunters would show up at night, turn on the floodlights on top of their truck and start shooting. It was all rather frightening, as there was no way for them to know people were living there and could have been shot. Even so, it must have been wonderful for her to let the children run and play freely in the fresh air and sunlight. What a relief to be in her own place, such as it was, away from Frank's criticism!

By fall, Paula and her children moved out to Cedar Valley, as well, filling the trailer to capacity. Frank eventually brought out a stove and propane to fuel it, but the mothers often ran out of propane before the next supply came. They were completely dependent on their husband, who had no concept of their needs. This would become a way of life for those who were assigned to the property. They were left abandoned and alone. A pit was dug, and an outhouse built, but with so little water, there was only essential personal hygiene.

The men in the Order had committed their time on Saturdays to go to the Cedar Valley property to begin work on what was to be the first of several homes. They would also use this opportunity to bring food and water to the women and children living there.

Eventually, a building was partially erected. It was roofed with tar paper and framed with particle board to form rooms which were on the second floor, accessible only by a ladder. This allowed our two mothers to spread out a little, while another family occupied the trailer where all meals were still prepared.

Two months before Helen and Paula moved into the building, another man moved his wife and their eight children to the Cedar Valley property to live in the trailer with our family. They were absolutely packed in there, making life unbearable. Paula was assigned to start teaching school as well as cook the meals.

To give an idea of how difficult things were for the mothers at this time, I am including portions of a note one of them sent me:

> *"I almost hesitate to write to you because I have been so miserable since I have been here. I'm afraid my note will be nothing but a complaint. I am writing*

anyway because I feel I need to express myself to someone. I hope for things to improve because I don't see how things could get much worse. There has got to be a day when things will improve. Frank has told us to keep the children indoors now and the building has been so cold since it has snowed (except for sleeping under many blankets), so we have sixteen children and three adults in one trailer. The noise and confusion is terrible, I have been asked to oversee the cooking as well as holding some kind of school. It gets dark around here early and we have been out of kerosene for a week now. We don't have any washing facilities for clothes or children. My baby has a sore bottom from the lack of laundry, but someone was able to go into town to do some diapers yesterday, so that will help. I am sending this list to you in the hopes Frank will buy these much-needed items. Vicks for congested chests, lotion [tons] for dry skin and sore bottoms, a wind-up clock to help us keep track of the time. At least we are safe and have all our children. I really don't mean to worry you because things have got to improve. I do love you. Thank you."

This broke my heart. These women were living in deplorable conditions. I felt guilty because I was working and living in town with access to the very things they were deprived of. They truly had and still do have my deepest respect and admiration.

Times worsened for them. One man was appointed to bring food to them in the form of "greens." As it turned out, he was "skimming off the top" the better items. Staples such as rice, beans, pasta or oatmeal were never purchased for them. They simply had to make do. Rarely was there any milk, eggs or cooking oil to ease their burden. They were in survival mode.

Frank had begun to move the bottled food we had in storage to the property, but he made it very clear that it was not to be used for everyday use. It was for some future catastrophe, apparently. But what was worse than now? Eventually, after being forced to feed the family two meager meals daily, the mothers realized they could no longer survive this way and began to utilize the bottled food. Being forced to disobey their husband, the wives received the brunt of his harsh disapproval.

Meanwhile, I worked early hours at the bookstore and after obtaining a sitter with someone in the Order, I worked for a staffing agency as a CNA (certified nurse's assistant) at various hospitals in the Salt Lake Valley. I would take a bus from downtown to which ever hospital I was assigned to for a 3-11 shift. Transportation was a nightmare and was a constant frustration as I had to arrange my own way home. Forced to solicit a ride, I would talk to people on the floor to see if anyone lived near me.

If that failed, I would tell the house supervisor that some emergency had come along and ask if she could help find a ride. Lucky for me, I would be sent to different hospitals, so people were not as likely to remember me and my constant transportation problems. Not having money to give for gas didn't help things, either. Late at night, after all day away from them, I would kneel by my sleeping little ones and tell them that I loved them so very much and that this wouldn't go on for long. But it did for years.

By the new school year, Frank had obtained an old Suburban to transport a couple of mothers and the school age children to the group's private school in Bluffdale. It would be packed with half of our collective children as they made their way into town several times a week. At the scene of an accident at the turn off to the school once, an officer was heard to say that he was glad it wasn't that Suburban filled with women and children. So much for being invisible! Frank never could seem to understand that it was because of our crowded and inadequate circumstances that state entities became involved with our family. They were not just out to get us.

Two of our mothers lived at that property while Grace, Betty and I were in town. Months later, my older children were sent to live at the Cedar Valley property, leaving me with my baby in town. It was so hard to be separated from them and they could not understand why it was so. I never worried about their care, since I knew that Paula and Helen would treat them well. I just missed my little ones.

With my children living in Cedar Valley, I began to accompany the work crew on Saturdays to be near them for a day or two over the weekend. It was such a short time to be with my little ones and leaving was awful. Each week would seem interminably long. Then, at last, would come some comfort. Sometimes, Frank would sleep over at the Cedar Valley property, which was a bonus for me, as I could spend more time with my children.

At the beginning of this time, before my children were

sent to live there with Helen and Paula, I was left needing a place to live. Frank made arrangements such as they were, for me and my children to live with Josie, a single woman in the group. We stayed in her two-bedroom apartment. There really wasn't room for us. I slept on the far side of her king size bed and my children slept on the floor.

Josie's two children and my two oldest attended the private school three days a week and I was supposed to hold homeschool with the four children while Josie was at work during the day. The problem was that I worked the night shift, which meant that I couldn't get enough sleep and was a horrible wreck physically and emotionally.

At this point, Frank would come to the apartment once a week. He stayed with me in Josie's bed, while she slept on the couch. I suggested that he not come to see me as it put Josie out of her own bed and she must have been uncomfortable with us both in her bed, but he would not hear of it. Again, he had to be in control and he would not take suggestions from any of us.

Josie was letting it be known to the rest of the group that I was living off her. It was really embarrassing, but true. Frank never gave her money. He did not understand that I was exhausted because of the commitment I was in and he was very upset that I would think of him changing his routine for my own comfort.

That time with Josie gave me a clearer understanding of how Helen must have felt for many, many years. She was constantly put in an embarrassing situation to suit our husband's lack of care, forcing her to live off other people's income. Once the Order came into being, we did this more and more. We became a burden on other people, while Frank remained unemployed.

A pall moved over the Cedar Valley property effort when, one day, some children playing with matches started a fire in the open downstairs part of the house. It could not be contained, and the structure burned to the ground.

All that work and sacrifice for nothing! But I was not sorry to see it go. I remember the mother of those children saying that God doesn't allow houses to burn down just to teach children not to play with matches. I think that God put a stop to that mess.

24

THE JUBILEE

————◦•◦————

ON A COLD GREY morning in October 1982, we hurriedly prepared breakfast and gathered the food we'd previously prepared for the day. It was time for the "Jubilee," a ritual Frank had found in the Old Testament and had decided to revive for the Order.

Helen, Paula and I bundled our children and gathered blankets for the long, cold drive as the heater in the car was still broken. There could be no rolling back into bed after prayers this Saturday morning. There would be brushing teeth, combing hair, and several layers of clothing as it would be cold at the property where a perpetual wind blew. I gathered a stack of cloth diapers and plastic covers for my babe; some mothers had two in diapers. It never hurts to over pack with as many children as we had.

Frank moved about the complex like a general marshaling an army. Finally, all were assembled, including those who did not live at the pink house. All had arrived and were ready for deployment. The entire Order—men, women and children—were going to the Cedar Valley property to observe an ancient but no longer practiced Jewish tradition, the Jubilee.

Frank was heavily influenced by Old Testament teachings, especially the Hebrew language and customs. Hence, this was his attempt to observe the concept of Jubilee. He had a very bright mind, and he would spend hours, which became years, studying Hebrew words, their roots and application, and retreating into the ancient past. There he seemed to find sanctuary—cocooned, shrouded, protected from the present—that part of time in which he seemed unwilling and unable to live.

We formed a caravan of cars and trucks with instructions to follow closely and to pull over, in case the driver lost sight of the vehicle behind him. We made our way to Camp Williams Road. Then, we drove beyond the Lehi turn off, continuing past farms, homes and the plant where a man in the Order had been killed in an explosion the year previous. The narrow-paved road ran parallel to Utah Lake. It was a monotonous and long journey. Soon we saw the huge metal towers which would soon carry electricity to great distances and had an ominous look to them.

After many miles, we turned off the main road and followed an unpaved, barely discernible road. It was little more than a trail. We were bouncing, bumping, and jostling over rocks and into ruts worn by some service vehicles and rabbit hunters.

Finally, we reached the last turn off, which was more

like a road, yet unpaved. Over a few rises, there it was, the Cedar Valley property with the run-down trailer on it and the ashes of the home we had begun but would never build again. We piled out of the vehicles, grateful to stretch our legs as children ran for the freedom of sage brush. They were kicking up a trail of dust, much to Frank's chagrin.

The custom of Jubilee had a special impact on the ownership and management of land in ancient Israel. The fiftieth year dealt largely with land, property and property rights. In Leviticus it says that it is a time of celebration of freedom, when everyone will receive back their original property, and slaves will return home to their families. Frank had managed to tweak the concept of forgiving debt to get himself out of debt which was the result of a big hospital bill. He had refused to seek assistance from the hospital or the state, so the total debt came to thousands of dollars. He said that the head of the Order should be the one to be free of debt first. There was talk of getting other men out of debt, but I don't think the Order held together long enough for that to happen.

Part of the Jubilee ceremony was for the men, heads of families, to walk and mark the boundaries of the property, marking each corner with a pile of stones. One of the men brought a goat out for the observance, but it never came back.

If the property was to remain viable, it was clear that there had to be a ready supply of water. Eventually a water diviner had been hired and a location for a well had been chosen. A drilling company had also been hired. But after drilling deeper than expected to find a moderate flow of water, the well had been capped to await a pump. As part of the Jubilee, we all lined up to receive a ceremonial sip of the brown, unfiltered well water. Frank lowered a small container secured by a cord into the pipe. This made the container with water easy to retrieve. He seemed to enjoy the pomp and circumstance of this type of thing.

I imagine most people would find all this ceremony very odd, but it was just how things were for us. There was not enough room in the trailer, so we gathered outdoors for a discourse Frank delivered about going into the wilderness as did the ancient Israelites to flee the evils of the day. We were to follow their example to be a righteous people. His vision was so clouded by his fascination with the old patriarchs that he wasbecoming disconnected from real life. What part of this was supposed to make sense?

There was also a ceremony of burying the hatchet. We were all to symbolically cast any hard feelings about any other into the hole containing a hatchet which was then filled in. The men built a fire and we sat around eating our evening meal, visiting and wondering how on earth Frank thought we could pull off all the things he had been talking about. This was so typical—some nebulous thought with no practical way to bring it to fruition.

25

BUTTERFIELD CANYON

⌖

ONCE WE RECEIVED WORD that the pink house was sold, and we had to move, a massive removal of all the additions that we'd made to the house swung into action. All the lumber and even the wood burning stove from Helen's shed were moved to the Cedar Valley property. It was not a small undertaking. Meanwhile, some men were appointed the task of finding somewhere that all the families could move to. It would preferably be all on one site, away from prying eyes.

They found a large property at the mouth of Butterfield Canyon which fit the bill. The land was owned by the Kennecott Mining Company, and had been previously leased to a family of goat cheese makers. They had practiced their skill for many generations, but now the family was closing their business and agreed to sub-rent to us, meaning the Order, including all the buildings.

As we drove along the winding road, we came first to an old brick home that must have been at least seventy-five years old. It had propane for heating, a septic tank and running water. This was to become home for Helen, Paula and their children.

Next, was the store where the cheese was sold, and a garage which would be converted into living quarters for a family of three wives and their children.

Third, was a very nice double-wide trailer home for another large family. This was to provide bath and toilet facilities for the family in the store/garage. It would also house the washer and dryer for the entire complex. Just outside of this building was propane for cooking and heating.

Last, was a single-wide trailer which was to be for myself and my children. There were two small bedrooms where my girls slept on bunks, while one son slept on the couch and my baby was with me in my room. The kitchen was small, with propane to cook and heat with, but nowhere for the dishwater to drain to, except outside. So, when I would do dishes, I would scoop out as much water as I could and then let the rest go down the drain. The bathroom was plumbed into the septic system. The following spring, Frank began to expand my trailer, even though we were only sub-renting.

Grace and Betty still lived at the yellow house, which also held Frank's library. But, by spring of 1982, Nelly had left Frank and moved to a different state, abandoning her eight children to the state to be placed in foster homes. All the mothers said that we would take the children and raise them with our own, but the courts would not allow it. We would have had to take two or three each, but at least we could have kept the children near each other. Paula officially applied to the court to raise the children, but was unsuccessful.

Butterfield Canyon was a wonderful place to live, notwithstanding the housing difficulties that went with it. There was room for the children to run and the air was clear, though the water was undrinkable as arsenic leached into our well from the mine tailings from the Bingham Mine. All the earth that had been sifted through for minerals was dumped aside and piled up on site.

The first of the copper mines was a short distance west of our homes, with the tailings spilling over the side. The large, famous, enormous, open pit mine lay only a few miles to the northwest of us. From time to time, there would be talk of the mine closing. This did not seem very likely because, along with copper, they were getting a lot of other precious metals out of it. Inevitably someone would make a comment about the closing rumor to the effect that—not to worry, someone must fill in that big hole, and it would take years! It is an enormous pit.

There were many small, weathered, wooden sheds around the house and trailers, one of which held a huge copper vessel that was previously used to heat the goat milk as part of the cheese making process. You could feel the history of generations past passing on the skill of making cheese as they did in their native country.

There were other small weathered structures that were

perhaps bunk houses for hired hands along the well-worn trails which intrigued the children and were quickly claimed for club houses.

Further up the hill was an old chicken coup. One of the men bought some chickens, since his family had raised them when he was a child. Not everyone was allowed in the coop for obvious reasons. Even the job of cleaning out the coop had to be earned. It was a real novelty to our children. We had never had chickens before that.

Many happy hours were spent by the children exploring the sage brush covered expanse around our new refuge. Some would bring home a variety of wild flowers. Some caught bugs while others would find the skeletal remains of goats or a variety of rocks as they experienced the joys of exploration. You would think they had found gold. I had a difficult time convincing them that iron pyrite was not gold or silver; they were so sure it was. There were pinion pines among the sage brush and further up the hill were dense stands of aspen. The air was clear and filled with the fragrance of pine. I was oblivious to the fact that there were mountain lions in the high country.

Early one cool, misty morning, I opened the door of the trailer and there stood the most magnificent buck I have ever seen. He slowly turned his head, holding huge antlers adding to his majesty. His soft brown eyes seemed to meet mine as he turned his head in the most dignified manner. I couldn't help telling him how beautiful he was and to stay there as I wouldn't hurt him. Slowly he turned and walked away, probably thinking that he could have trampled me or gored me and that I should stay where I was. It was one of those magical moments when you understand that we are all God's creation.

We would see groups of deer grazing in fields close to the canyon, oblivious to the sound of cars driving on the roadway or the squealing of, "There's a deer," from the children. There was a sheep farm by the turnoff to the canyon and spring time was a festival of lambs so frisky and woolly, our children wanting to hold them. It was during this time that I got word that my father had died. I was still feeling the loss of my son very deeply when one day, I felt as though Daniel was showing Dad where I was. It was just a feeling, but it was very comforting.

A similar experience occurred once when I was at work. I could smell propane gas there, so I called home to ask one of the mothers to go check on my children. My oldest daughter had just come into the trailer. Upon smelling the gas, she had turned it off. They went outside until the gas cleared. It was nice to know we were being watched over.

Winter had its own adventures. One sunny afternoon, many of the children were playing outdoors. There was a lot of snow that year in the canyon and the boys had ventured into some deep snow a fair distance from the trailers. Several of the children came bursting through the door, calling to me, saying that my son Ben was stuck in the snow and couldn't get out. He had walked on some ice encrusted snow and fallen through, stuck up to his chest and unable to move.

Racing behind the boys, I exhausted myself just getting to him. He was so cold and crying, "Mom get me out of here."

Breaking through the crust, I was able to pull him out, shivering and soaked through. His feet were so cold, it hurt him to try to walk, so I packed him out on my back. Once home, I began to warm his hands and feet in luke-warm water; then slowly with warmer water. I knew not to rub his skin or use a heating pad. He slowly warmed. Feeling and color returned to his feet, but they still hurt. It really shook me up, but he was fine.

A headcount of sorts: Our three mothers and our children, twenty in number, one man with his three wives and their eleven children who lived in the shop and converted garage and one man with his wife and their five children in the double wide trailer. They were supposed to be an interface between all of us and the outside world.

Frank had not been gainfully employed for years and spent virtually all of his time at the yellow house. When we would ask him for money for gasoline, greens, paper products, cleaning agents, or anything, he would straighten himself up, hold his head up and say, "Well, I don't have any money." There was no apology, no explanation, no shame, just no money. It left you wondering what had just happened.

A sister wife who was also pushed to her limit got a job and kept her paycheck for herself. I had been a working mom for years, giving Frank my paycheck automatically. I remember years earlier, a bank manager calling me to be sure that it was all right to deposit my paychecks in to Frank's account. He didn't know Frank was my husband.

"Oh yes," I replied, "it's convenient for me."

I was fine with helping the family, but once I realized

it was a possibility, I soon followed my sister wife's choice. At first, I felt guilt-ridden and sick to my stomach when I stopped handing my checks over. The chute had been greased for a long time now as some very hurtful truths came into focus: I finally realized that I had little value outside of the bedroom and a paycheck. This is also the time I sent my children to the group private school and was left to find a way to pay for their tuition.

One of the men living at Butterfield Canyon wanted to have all his family live at the canyon, so I was moved to a trailer home in Bluffdale across from the polygamist meeting house which was around a fourteen-mile drive. It was wonderful; such an improvement. It had water we could drink, two working bathrooms and a kitchen sink that connected to the sewage line. There were two bedrooms at one end of the trailer with a bathroom, washer and dryer hook up and a back door. The kitchen opened to the living room.

At the opposite end of the trailer was my room and another room for my boys. There was also a cellar dug with shelves for storage. There was tons of room to play, including a tree house which my boys expanded on. After a while, I also bought a trampoline. We had it on the grass, under a big Chinese elm tree. I found out later that the children would climb the tree and bail out onto the trampoline where they would jump and bounce to their content.

Inside, there was a wonderful wood burning stove for heating, but the owner needed it for his own family. So he took it and I had to find something else to keep us warm. I looked in the nickel adds for a wood burning stove I could afford and managed to get it home. Frank hooked it up to the pipe. But there was no wood easily accessible here. During the winter, I scrounged wood from wherever I could, including dragging home wood pallets. Those things are hard to chop.

One evening in winter, I noticed a small hole in the back of the stove which made me nervous, as I would heavily load it to try to have it last through the night, especially in the dead of winter. We'd rehearsed how to get out of the trailer and where to meet if there were a fire. Everyone knew not to go back in no matter what. Each night, I would pray that we would be safe or that we would all get out or pass together.

From here, we could walk to school and church which was very helpful. One day I found some wallpaper in a bin and decided to put it on part of the wall in the kitchen. Purchasing some glue, I proceeded to apply it to the wood panels. Pleased with the improvement, I was doing dishes when I heard a kind of crackling sound. I couldn't tell what it was until I turned around and noticed the paper peeling off the wall. Undaunted, I found a stapler and stapled that paper to the wall!

Speaking of walls, I do not think there was an ounce of insulation in them at night. When the house was still, I could hear mice scratching in the walls where they must have taken up residence—especially in the fall. I would set traps, but they were too smart to get caught, I guess.

Later, the fire department, which came to do inspections on the meeting house, declared my trailer to be a death trap and it was condemned. The council had been disgusted with Frank for a long time, especially for his lack of support of his family and the fact that he refused to get a job. He would not take direction or guidance from the group's leaders. As a result, I was moved into a home closer to town. By then, I was divorced from Frank, which I will explain later. I lived in this new home for years, and very much appreciated having the opportunity.

26

PRETENSE

————◇•◆•◇————

THERE WAS MOST DEFINITELY a penchant among men of a particular mind set, especially among some of Frank's followers, to seclude their families in remote areas such as the Cedar Valley or the west desert of Utah. These were truly desolate places with no utilities or running water, with run down trailer homes that were totally isolated from civilization. As with the Cedar Valley property, these families tried to avoid discovery by the government. Living in desolate places was supposed to make them invisible, but there was always uncertainty. The uncertainty extended to survival. These families lived suspended between worlds, merely subsisting while husbands lived in town looking for jobs, with little success. I wondered sometimes how hard the men were looking. As with Frank, they seemed indignant when forced to move their families to better circumstances.

Other men purchased land in Utah County, attempting to draw less attention to the many large families that would live there. Only those who were approved could build on that land, providing a buffer between them and the outside world. To their credit, these were nice homes with utilities and sewage. The men here held steady jobs, as did many of the women, living so as not to draw attention to themselves. Eventually, the land around them was developed into subdivisions, and they had to leave, as was inevitable.

Still, the ideal of living off the grid continues in isolated clusters of people who feel they could defend themselves if need be against whatever disasters might hit them, without the need of government intervention. You hear of people building shelters for a future doomsday event. Then they complain bitterly when they get a property tax bill, or the health department wants to look things over. They don't seem to understand that there's no way to live in complete isolation today, surrounded by other communities.

There was a time when I completely bought into this ideal of isolation from the government, doing all that I could to support my husband, which just goes to show that it only had to make sense at the time!

27

SECRECY AND INUENDOS

———◦◆◦———

THERE HAS ALWAYS BEEN a sense of secrecy surrounding polygamy, I suppose because it's illegal. At the time I joined the group, a greater number of members had been raised in that way of life. Their parents and grandparents had been persecuted and some sent to jail for their beliefs. After Helen and Nelly's dad was released from jail, he was ordered not to continue in the polygamist lifestyle, meaning he had to choose one wife with whom to live. He was not about to do that and moved his family to other states, and even as far away as old Mexico, as it was referred to, where there was a colony of polygamists.

The story goes that, in the United States, he was moving one family to another location under the cover of night, the car was loaded with his family and their belongings when he rolled out of the driveway, headlights off so as not to draw attention to himself. A short way down the road, he turned the car lights on, only to see that there was a car behind him that also turned its lights on. He was being followed. Such stories of government surveillance were told and retold. It had a way of immortalizing those who had experienced real imprisonment and persecution in the past, as well as creating and solidifying distrust of the legal system and outsiders.

In the late fifties, into the early sixties, a division of loyalties occurred within the original body of polygamous fundamentalists over who should be the leader, resulting in what became known as the split. This divided many families, causing a great rift between brothers and sisters, as well as long-time friends. A large number rejoined those still living in Short Creek, Arizona and Hildale, Utah, now known as the Fundamentalist Church of Latter-day Saints. The rest remained with the AUB, or Apostolic United Brethren. Of course, both groups of fundamentalists claimed to have the "real" authority to perform plural marriages and hold religious keys passed down from the early days of the church.

This distinction, at some point, turned into a sense of exclusivity, particularly for those who had been "faithful" to their group for a long time. In turn, this made it difficult for newcomers to feel welcome, often being looked upon with suspicion. Our family was not well accepted in our group on several levels. It was partly because Frank was a convert, but it was also because he was secretive and aloof. Additionally, two of his wives were the children of a family in the group whose mother was considered incompetent, to put it kindly. We were also very poor, which was something Frank took great pride in. We were all but sequestered, except to go to work. Even the wives who had family in the group were not permitted to visit with them. I think this gave the impression that there was something to hide; which as it turned out, there was mostly the autocratic way Frank ruled his family and how little they subsisted on.

The council, which is the governing body of the group, had never been of one mind or purpose. Each member would create his own following, a sub-culture, though none of them would admit to it. By the time I came into the family, Frank had been called to the council, but was not well accepted or respected by his peers. He countered this by creating his own select group of followers who fell prey to the concept of being intellectually superior. Therefore, they were more spiritually advanced, of course. In polygamy, regardless of an individual's alliance, the constant is that a man is to rule over his wives, which can be a recipe for disaster.

28

SEDUCTION OF A DANGEROUS KIND

———◦◆◦———

THERE IS SOMETHING SEDUCTIVE about the idea that you, as a man, are a part of a select few, chosen to live the highest laws of God and to receive the attendant rewards. Such enticement left virtually no man untouched. When he is extended this much power, it is a short step to exercising unrighteous dominion over his family. Even if he doesn't intend it, he can quickly run amuck.

It is one thing to be intoxicated by newfound power, but a different thing to take it to the extreme of regarding your wives as property, much like a pot or pan. A few men set upon an equally dangerous path, judging that one wife or another was not worthy to have a child until she became more obedient to him. It is worse yet when that woman is shamed and embarrassed publicly as it becomes widely known. Young men married once are told to take another wife within a year or the first wife "will ruin your life" as she will like being the only wife and resist him taking any more wives, assuming she has that much influence.

Frank held a cottage meeting every Monday night and it became an elaborate affair. This ritual was during the time of the bookstore. On Monday afternoon, I was to call whomever Frank had chosen, to ask if they wanted to have the meeting in their home that evening. It was a compliment to be chosen and no one ever said no, even if they sounded a little inconvenienced. Having set a location, I was then to call all the people on Frank's list and inform them of that location, creating an air of being somewhat clandestine. All of this was a well-orchestrated plan, creating a sense of privilege and secrecy in that they were being specifically included.

These meetings continued to be well attended for many years, though Frank sifted out those who would not follow him completely. Each Monday night, Frank expounded on some religious subject or another while those in attendance hung on every word. Frank had a gifted mind and carefully used words to ensure a following. He was a master of using innuendo to convince others he knew the secret to all mysteries, theology and exactly how to run a family. Eventually, only the people in his following were invited to these meetings.

The stage was being well set for absolute commitment to him. Adding to the sense of exclusivity was Frank's assurance that if a man was a faithful follower, he would be made privy to unfolding fulfillment of prophecy or impending catastrophes. One of these prophesies was that when it was time to leave the Salt Lake Valley, as in the case of an apocalypse of some kind, only those selected by Frank would be notified. Under the cover of darkness, they would be picked up in a bus and quietly leave town. It was a powerful way to use fear.

Frank taught about a secret password, which was circulated among the Order, which made me very uneasy. It was like watching the Pied Piper leading the children along, only to take them to the edge of a cliff. Looking back, I think Frank needed to see himself in an elevated station. He worked hard to create followers, assuring those below him, that following him would be a qualifying commitment in God's eyes for those in the Order. It was a way of nurturing followers along through the channel of classes and teachings into the deeper waters of a United Order type community.

The fisherman's net will harvest a variety of fish—some good, some not so much, and some even fatal. So, it would prove with Frank's net. Among his followers, there was a variety of personalities with different strengths. For the most part, they were good people impressed with his teachings. However, one man proved treacherous.

Tom was a man who ruled over his family in severity. He broke each one of them down emotionally, then convinced them that he was the only one who truly loved them. Not surprisingly, they were stubbornly loyal to him. Clouded by fear, they were unable to think for themselves since he dictated their every move. What Frank could do with words, Tom did with his brand of control. Tom would prove to be unreliable and tire of employment quickly, resorting to dishonest practices to obtain money. After a series of offenses, including spending rent money on the Butterfield Canyon property, he would kneel on one knee and ask Frank for forgiveness in front of the Order, usually in a Monday night meeting in front of us.

Frank tolerated years of this type of behavior because he thought he could help Tom straighten up and become reliable. But when Tom's confessions became serious enough to include spying on some of Helen's daughters through a peep hole, while they were in the shower. Frank was finally forced to tell Tom that he had to leave the Order.

Tom vanished, not unlike a tornado, having spent itself with all its fury, leaving a trail of destruction behind. He and his family moved to another town. I don't think I have seen him since. I would have said, "good riddance," but I felt sorry for Tom's wife; she was a mild woman, though fiercely loyal to Tom.

There were many attracted to Frank's net who were new to the world of polygamy, inexperience being their only offense. It might have been funny watching these men test the waters among our daughters had it not been the look of hesitancy and a little sadness in the eyes of each man's first wife. These men were both hopeful and hindered by Frank's habit of luring newcomers by extending the intimation that he had a daughter for them.

Several times, while living at the pink house, Frank had one of the men conduct a social with a dance so that the families could interact informally. Regardless of group dances held once a month for the rest of the Order, Frank insisted that his own family could not attend. We could only attend the dances that Frank set up. During one of these socials, he made the statement that he wanted our daughters to marry these new brethren.

(Bear in mind that these men were in their thirties and the oldest of our daughters was only fifteen and had not completed high school.)

At Frank's dances, these men acted like kids in a candy store, their mouths watering as they stared at our daughters. Remarkably absent in any of Frank's conversations were any comments regarding our son's future in living the principle of plural marriage. Frank seemed only to find value in the leverage our daughters provided to ensure a following of committed men.

One newly converted man really caught the vision. Once he received consent to get to know any one of our daughters, with the injunction that he would have to wait for marriage as they were all still too young, he seemed to decide that he might be able to manage a twofer and get the fifteen-year-old daughter and my thirteen-year-old daughter.

Not realizing the danger he was placing his wife in, this man sent her to become best friends with the thirteen-year-old, to better his chances with her. I could see exactly what was going on and with the fury of a mother bear, I ran the wife off, leaving no doubt that my daughter was off limits.

The man later had the nerve to complain to Frank about my behavior, so when confronted with the incident,

I said, "Yes, I made it clear that this was getting out of hand; that I didn't like those tactics." The fact that he was so ambitious to try to line up two young girls at the same time and that he sent his wife to influence my young and impressionable daughter with apparent friendship.

A little taken aback Frank said, "That's my job, to run them off, not yours."

"Just so you do," was my reply. Before long, this man left without any of our daughters.

Another man used shameless flattery on Frank to gain favor and was given consent to "get to know" one of the Order's girls without her mother's knowledge. Seeing him holding her hand in a very long hand shake, the mom quickly pulled her child aside. Not to worry, with lightning speed he turned his attention to another girl, trying to appear most solemn and dignified though he was like a child, pretending that he didn't care his chosen toy was taken away.

It was disgusting to me, the way these men hung on Frank's every word as if it came from God himself. He certainly encouraged their slavish attitude toward him. To quote this same flattering man, when the subject of building homes and forming a community in a desolate part of the Cedar Valley was presented to the Order, "Brother Frank, you be our Moses and we will support you."

That was a trap loaded for bear! Frank had not been gainfully employed for years. We had only my small income while we were being supported by the Order. Frank was absolutely all right with the situation, using other men's vehicles to get greens and not pay for gas. We were just using everyone and everything. It was hard to hold my head up.

But instead of being embarrassed by this, Frank saw himself as some ancient patriarch, living at the wrong time. The man who thought Frank was his "Moses" fortified Frank in his beliefs with his words. Our husband gave us little more than the time he spent in our beds. He gave even less time to our children. Now, the Order was siphoning off what was left.

29

FAMILY COUNCIL

FAMILY COUNCIL WAS A marathon emotional event held every Sunday afternoon, lasting several hours. The older girls would tend the smaller children while the adults met. No one could escape or outrun the council. If a wife was sick in bed, we would meet in her room. If you were in labor, it still caught up with you.

Things could yet ugly in the council. One of earliest experiences was shortly after I was married. Nelly was hurling one hurtful insult after another at Paula, referring to her as 'that thing over there.' Helen hung her head and I sat there with my mouth hanging open. I had never witnessed such nastiness and felt sorry for Paula. No matter what had passed between them previously, she did not deserve to be treated like that. The source of Nelly's venom was never explained to me and Frank made only feeble efforts to calm Nelly down.

Over the years, nothing much changed about the council. The agenda was predictable. There were housing adjustments, questions about which of Helen's girls would be sent to Nelly's home to tend her children that week and which of her boys she needed a break from. Frank seemed to think it was necessary to send one of our children as an exchange, but none of the other wives wanted to send them. Of course, Frank prevailed and off would go one of them of his choosing. This trading around of our children was in part to appease Frank trying to enforce his generic mother rule, meaning we were to think of each other's children as dearly as we did our own. But mostly it was Nelly unable to handle the children she had and kept having.

We wives had little influence on our husband's decisions in or out of the council. Really, the meeting itself was a dismal review of our circumstances such as how little income there was with a review of what was expected financially of each of the mothers for the week to come. We discussed the details of Nelly's and my work schedule, how could we work transportation that type of thing. At one point, I would go to the bookstore in the morning and take a bus to whatever hospital I was to work at. The older girls were to step in to help tend the younger children left behind.

On one occasion, as time for girls' camp drew near, we were told that some of the girls could go, but one or two would have to stay home to help the mothers. Each of our daughters had been so excited about going that the idea of any of them being forced to stay home seemed cruel. As if on cue, Paula and I both said that we didn't need help and wanted all to go.

Frank must have been caught off guard at this, but all the girls went to camp that year. It was worth the reprimand Paula and I received about sustaining our husband and obeying him instead of deciding things on our own. In that moment, recollection washed over me as I caught a glimpse of the capable, independent woman I used to be and perhaps still was. I just needed to let her into the light of day more often.

There was another time when Tom, one of the men in the Order who had been asking to marry one of Helen's daughters for over a year, sat with his wife in our family meeting. We were surprised and didn't know what was going on at first. This was the man who recklessly spent the money given to him by the Order to make a payment on the canyon property and had been a peeping Tom. No pun intended, it was his name. He had also stalked the girl he wanted to marry and would sneak around the house and trailers to watch her.

In council, Frank asked us our opinion of this marriage. I wasn't only shocked that he asked our opinion, but that he was even considering the possibility of allowing such a marriage. I threw caution to the wind. It took a lot of courage as I had a run-in with Tom a few times and was intimidated by him. I said that I didn't think he was reliable enough to marry our daughter or anyone else's. It was harsh, but other wives agreed in varying degrees. Any girl who married him would have lived in deplorable circumstances while having one baby after another. Tom stared me down, but I couldn't go along with it.

Family council often included a skillful dance of words, with Frank emphasizing the need to grow our number of wives. In his mind, numbers counted, because a larger polygamous family was supposed to make us more acceptable to God, not to mention impressing his peers. To gain another wife would fill his next quorum, making five of us.

As luck would have it, occasionally, a single woman would find her way from the 'outside' into the tangled world of polygamy. So, it was with Francine. Once she came into view, the wives romanced her with great enthusiasm, inviting her into our home. Meanwhile, Frank as instructor of mysteries, maintained a respectable distance.

What were we thinking?! We were trying to please our husband of course! While we were accustomed to being poor, living in crowded, inadequate conditions and eating out of dumpsters, she was not. As incredulous as it seemed to Frank, Francine married elsewhere. Most of the wives were disappointed. But, for Frank, the sting of rejection took on a dimension of its own. He withdrew further into his private, delusional world, if that was possible. With the passage of time, we would find it was indeed possible.

More than once after that, I was sent to "get to know" some single woman, often a young one maybe seventeen years old or so. I was not much for small talk, not much of a conversationalist and never knew what to say. I would feel so foolish as I had no doubt they knew what I was up to. Maybe I should have cut right to it and said that I was there to see if she wanted to marry my husband. It should have been a simple answer, yes or no, and at least that way I would have been out of my misery. But that wasn't the way that it worked. It was always so complicated, as Frank wanted to grow his reputation and power.

During another family council, Frank dropped a bomb of historic proportion. He wanted us to agree to his marrying Helen's daughter, Sharon. Helen had been married to a man in the group who had beaten her, thus allowing her to be released from him. The poor woman traded a man who physically beat her for one who abused her mentally and emotionally. Sharon was from the first marriage and therefore not Frank's biological child, making her fair game for him according to the rules of polygamy.

How could a woman of child-bearing years be anything but breeding stock to Frank? What a repugnant thought, the idea that the person Sharon knew only as her father would become her husband with all the intimacy that goes with it. I can't imagine what that would have done to her mentally or emotionally. What better way than to marry a child so as to speak and raise her to be the devoted, obedient wife you wish her to be? It would have been such a disgusting and distasteful destination for such an innocent girl.

Sharon was only thirteen at the time and although the nuptials would not occur until she was sixteen or so, the agreement Frank wanted meant she would have been sequestered from any possible suitors for the next three years. What a horrific fate would have awaited if we had gone along with it. Fortunately, none of the mothers agreed with the proposition, shattering Frank's aspirations. I think it is fair to say that this episode distanced all of us from him for a long time. Frank behaved like a petulant child, pouting over our decision, but we could not relegate this child to such a fate. As it turned out, Sharon was married off to a close friend of Frank's who was twice her age, solidifying an alliance.

As the years passed, the weekly meeting became a constant review of our hopeless financial condition with an update on the current financial pipe dream that we were all hanging our hopes on. Frank seemed to attract men who had grand ideas of making money with no real work attached. One was when Glenn suggested a tax shelter scheme. He would set up a dummy corporation on paper and Frank would supposedly receive an income for running the business, as well as running costs and payroll for it. It was to be a tax shelter.

Evidently, it was to be an elaborate affair, not to mention that it was probably illegal. The mothers would most likely have been listed as employees. Who knows how much trouble we could have gotten into! Some of us joked about jail time sounding pretty good as we could have used the rest. The reality could have been devastating! Yet we were so desperate that this seemed the answer to our financial woes. As a result, we prayed for it to happen and it was on our minds most of the time. What a waste of energy.

Glenn was also interested in living plural marriage. He was a married man, but his wife would have nothing to do with plural marriage. She was an educated woman and held a great job. They had a fine family and were well connected in the community. Glenn would have conversations with Frank at the bookstore, some of which were impossible not to hear. Maybe I didn't try hard enough—*oh, well!*

One such conversation was when Glenn was lamenting

that his wife would not be persuaded to go along with him. Frank told him that there came a time when a man was justified in proceeding without his wife's consent. Frank said that it was too bad that the intelligent ones were so hard to teach.

It was hard not to react to that, but I wasn't included in the conversation and I didn't have the courage to say anything. After all, my sister wives and I were simple enough to have married Frank. Glenn soon found a woman and courted her. She agreed to become his second wife. I know this because I was witness to their marriage.

I don't know if she knew that his first wife didn't know about her, she probably didn't. This was a lovely woman who was kind and generous. She held a very good job and was accustomed to supporting herself. Yet Glenn took advantage of her vulnerability and spent little time with her. She was supposed to believe that she was sacrificing her feelings for the sake of keeping plural marriage alive. All while Glenn continued to live a full life with family and friends while the crumbs he threw her were supposed to be enough. He spent a few hours here and there, seeing her less and less and eventually not seeing her at all. She became disillusioned with his version of the principal and I suppose disgusted with him.

The saying that hindsight is twenty-twenty holds true for my life. In retrospect, Frank had placed himself on a pedestal and we wives did a great job of keeping him there for so long. It was what we were supposed to do as plural wives, but it encouraged the worst in him.

I have also come to realize that ours was scarcely a marriage, as we had a parent/child, not a husband/wife relationship. So it was with each wife. He was always in control, dictating our next move, always win/loose and never win/win. We pampered him when he was home and gave sympathy to alleviate what we perceived as guilt or embarrassment for not providing for his family.

On one occasion, he looked like a broken man and I felt sorry for him. I actually said the words, "Oh, but you give us the chance to live the law and give us our children."

Unbelievable! I totally validated his behavior. At that time, my baby was about six weeks old and I was trying to get my strength back. So I said that I would go back to work if he wanted me to. With that, he straightened himself up and said that he had never asked a wife to go to work nor would he. No, he guilted us into volunteering instead, and I walked right into it. Most families these days need two incomes and do what they must to make things work. But we didn't even have a full one income. Our husband did not work and he took from our income anyway.

30

UGLY THINGS

———◦•◦———

URING THE 1970S, THE serpent of child
molestation raised its ugly head among the
group. Evidently, this had been going on for a
long time, but the children were afraid to come forward.
There was no safe place for them as no one would have
believed them. The perpetrator was a long-time member
of the council and was supposed to be above reproach. The
children were living with the fear of the repercussions if
they were to tell, so the crimes continued. Even when they
did begin to come forward, the children were treated as if
there was something wrong with them for saying such a
thing.

No one wants such horror to be real and for a long time
the accusations were received with skepticism. The council
was sweeping it under the rug as the perpetrator adamant-

ly denied any wrong doing, calling the children liars. One child said that his father, the abuser, had threatened him with a knife if he told. This man was the father and grandfather of many of the victims. He chose the most vulnerable and weakest, so these children suffered without hope.

He was finally dropped from the council while continuing to proclaim his innocence. Some of his wives and children remained loyal to him, choosing to believe that he was the victim and had been treated wrongly. This man never admitted to his crimes before he died. I hope he died in his shame.

Disbelief rippled through the congregation as soon after, another council member stood to confess his wrongdoings and expressed sorrow to the disgrace of himself and his family. So many people looked up to him, even more than the first sexual predator, and I couldn't help wondering, "How bad can this get? How can this be happening? He will not be back!"

But this time the law was involved, and this community leader went to prison as the first one should have. What a waste of a person's life to become mired in such evil. What a tragedy for the children, who would have to deal with the consequences of what had been done to them the rest of their lives.

But the worst was yet to come as my own daughter and the daughter of a sister wife came forward with testimony of their father and others with him molesting them. This didn't come out until years after the fact. In fact, I had left Frank by that time, but for other reasons.

I feel such guilt that they bore that burden alone all

those years. After what happened with Sharon, how could I have not seen that something was wrong? My only answer is that I was rarely home. These fragile young women were called into a group court by the council, then asked for their testimony, which was treated with disdain and disbelief. Once again, they were the victims. Frank, was finally disfellowshipped for "unchristian-like" conduct.

Grace asked if she should be released from Frank but was told that she should stay with him. Frank could have returned to meetings but chose not to. He seemed to feel, as with Tom, that he had been treated unjustly. Neither Frank nor the wives who remained with him returned to church until after his death. There was a saying my grandmother used when speaking of such awful things and their consequences. She would say that bad deeds cast long shadows. It is old-fashioned but true. No one escaped the long shadow of Frank's bad deeds.

Some things, if you are not vigilant, remain unnoticed until they blindside you. This is how it has been with Franks unnatural propensity towards Sharon and even some of his own biological daughters. Alice had been close to her father, which was not typical, as Frank rarely allowed any of the children to become so. I should have seen it as a warning sign, but I didn't.

As Alice became of marriageable age and was paying serious attention to one of the men in the Order, Frank made an unnerving statement in family meeting. He said that before coming to this life, Alice had the choice of coming as his daughter or his wife, and she'd decided to come as his daughter.

It was the type of thing that made you wonder if you heard right. Why would he even bring this up, supposing that he really did have some miraculous way of knowing such a thing? Why on earth would he make such a stunning remark if it was not to confuse this girl?

True to his own selfish form, Frank then coached Alice in the possibility of being his wife in a way that could easily be denied by him if he was confronted openly. Always in secret, always veiled, using words that could be interpreted some other way. To the last minute, his most devoted and remaining wife told Alice that it was still possible for her to marry her father. Alice is not my daughter and choose not to state her mother's name.

This leaves no doubt in my mind that there was something seriously wrong in Frank's thinking, wanting to marry two daughters (Sharon and Alice) and molesting some others. It just is not acceptable in any way. I know that this type of thing goes on all over, but you never think it will happen to those close to you. This has been an awful thing to write about, but it had to be done. I couldn't look away from it as others did.

31

HOLDING ON

THERE COMES A TIME when you feel yourself spiraling into oblivion, so you grab onto anything in reach that offers the hope of slowing your descent. So, it has been for me from time to time, circling around only to see the abyss like water circling the drain. In each cycle, the water goes lower and lower so that you see only the darkness of the drain pipe before you.

At those times when I was still married to Frank, I would reach out to the few friends I was allowed to have, the ones I could trust to give me perspective. I would tell them that I didn't know how to hold on any longer, reciting the struggles that were my constant, "the way things were." I felt so overwhelmed, almost like trying to drag my world through deep water. I wondered, could this possibly be the way the 'law' was supposed to be lived? I would ask myself if I was just not good enough, not strong enough or dedicated enough? Was I so weak that I was not fit for the work and was this how people like myself were weeded out to be discarded at my own hand, by my own lack of worthiness?

Then there were times when I would pop to the surface like a cork or something lighter than water and I would gasp in the sweet fresh air of hope. I was thinking that somehow, from some unknown source, I would find new strength to understand the vision of what my husband was trying to accomplish. With this new hope in hand, I would set about shouldering the responsibility of making his desires come to pass, along with trying to be a good mother to my children. Then, as surely as one season follows another, I would find myself spiraling downward again.

It was on one of these descents that I spoke with a friend who was working for a family counselor. She suggested something that I was sure would send me straight to hell. She reasoned with me that I didn't possess the skills I needed to survive in my marriage and I knew she was right. So, with all the courage I could muster, I went to see this man on a free consultation. The rest I would have to pay for.

As we spoke, it became clear that he was a Christian man and that we held basic beliefs in common. I also had to level with him about being a plural wife. He didn't even flinch. We talked for a while and then he asked, "What feelings do you have when you think about your Savior or God?"

I replied, "I feel love, peace, joy, hope, calm, open and free."

"Okay," he continued, "How about when you think about your husband?" I wasn't expecting that.

However, I replied, "Fear, darkness, closed, hopeless, not loved or valued, anxious." The words came tumbling out, and I was unable to control them, like the rushing waters of melting snow in the spring time. I exhaled heavily.

He sat back in his chair and was quiet for a moment. "There is something I would like you to consider," he began. "There are always alternatives in life. Some may not be suitable at all. Some you may not choose. Some that would work and would be of benefit to you, but there are always alternatives."

In my world there were no alternatives. I asked myself, *Could this be true? Do I really have that autonomy?*

I thanked him and left, but never went back. How could I? I had no money. I also didn't tell Frank, but I held those encouraging words in my heart and mind as if they were jewels and I took them out from time to time to examine them. I allowed them to shine a light on my path going forward.

It is said that the definition of insanity is doing the same thing and expecting a different outcome. But in the polygamous world, one must never go to the outside to find answers. As a result, personal and family problems are never solved because the same answers are given over and over again.

Years after my experience with the family counselor, there was a huge disturbance over members of the group going to seminars such as Rising Star, was one of them, supposedly to help an individual find self-worth and value.

I never attended any, but it sounded like a lot of hoop-la to me. It was causing a division of opinion and loyalties, even though some of the council members and their families participated in them. No one wanted to lose control of their families. Still, the faithful held to the shunning of such things as they continued bumping around in the dark.

Around this time, I read M. Scott Peck's book, *The Road Less Travelled*. Probably not more than a week later, the book hit our "do-not-read" list. It was emphasized over the pulpit. Of course, we mustn't read it: Someone might think for themselves!

But, it was too late. I had already read it and was in the process of being able to take responsibility for my part in things I had seen myself as a victim in. The clouds were beginning to part. It was not easy going through the process to give up my "poor-victim" mentality. Now thankfully, I refuse to see myself in that light. I can learn from the past, but I will not allow it to have power over me, I will not live in its shadow.

To me, our creator is the source of all truth. This truth is in the very air we breathe. It freely flows about us. We have only to allow it into our lives. Even though change is difficult, it is very much worth it. It takes courage, just like breathing, you have to let all of the air out of your lungs in order to take the next breath.

32

MIDWIFE ASSISTANT

———◦•◦———

FRANCINE, WHO HAD CHOSEN not to marry Frank initially, was a certified midwife with patients in and out of the group. Frank had given me permission to visit with her. This might have been an errand to try to persuade her toward joining our family, as she was recently divorced. Whatever the intent might have been, it was so refreshing to me to spend time with her. On one of our visits, she said that she was looking for an assistant to go with her on births.

"If only it was possible," I told her. "I would love to be that person." And somehow, I was.

Throughout the year of 1981, I accompanied Francine on many deliveries. I was becoming a full time assistant, learning the details of monthly checkups and record keeping. It filled an empty spot in my life.

I would be responding to the call of a mother in labor, sometimes in the middle of the night, staying until she was delivered. What a wonderful experience it was to be part of the miracle of birth and to watch Francine work with the mom. She was soothing, encouraging, and guiding, even being firm with the mother to bring her babe into the world.

One of the most amazing things I have ever witnessed was with Francine on one particular delivery. The couple lived in the Heber Valley, a good hour's drive from home. We knew that when she called us, we would be there until she delivered, because she wanted the support. This mom was mentally prepared for the experience of natural childbirth in a home setting. Labor was progressing slowly, so we all took a walk. We were soaking in the mountain air and beautiful surroundings to take our minds off things and perhaps hurry baby along.

After several hours, her labor progressed to where the mom was getting ready to begin pushing. There she was, lying on the bed with one foot against my hand as she pushed through a contraction. To say I was startled would be an understatement. There was her babe, presenting face up, motionless, eyes closed with good color as if he were asleep, peaceful and just waiting to be born.

Suspended in time, I thought what a sobering and impactful moment this was. There was no sense of urgency. The mom was just gathering her strength for the next contraction. With that came one shoulder as Francine skillfully rotated it around. The next contraction brought the babe. There was clamping, suctioning, dad cutting the cord, laughing and crying for joy. If that was not the definition of a miracle, I'd like to hear why!

I can remain calm through pretty much anything, but this experience put me to the test. I couldn't let on at the time, but seeing that baby's head out and motionless, well, suffice it to say, I put a loving smile on my face and shut my mouth. Anyone who has worked in labor and delivery knows that no matter what, you always act as though whatever is going on happens all the time, no sweat.

This experience has stayed in my mind for thirty years now and is as clear as the day it happened. The wonder of it still fills me with awe. How do you express an experience like that, so that someone else's hair stands on end too with the thrill of it, I don't think you can, not adequately. It is one of those moments when you realize with great clarity that you have been part of something that is much bigger than you are; that it has changed your life.

My journal entry for Wednesday, October 14, 1981:

This morning I asked Frank for some gas money, so I could do Francine's checkups. He said, "This is getting out of hand." I didn't know what he meant as it turned out, Nelly has been on a rampage over my working with Francine. He said that Nelly becomes enraged over me in this field. I offered to withdraw, and he said that was what he wanted me to do. I couldn't believe it; this family is completely run according to what she demands. He said that this is what the Lord wants me to do. I resented this so much. Why did she have to have everything? I guess she thinks Francine

will take her on deliveries now, but I know she won't.
I am embarrassed to say that I am happy she won't. I
still went to Francine's for an appointment.

This is not part of the journal entry but my view now: It was so like Frank to put things in a spiritual setting. I did not then, nor do I now, believe that it was God's will. Frank just knew that I would comply if he put it that way. I guess I can fall for anything.

My time with Francine prepared me to pinch hit a few times. One night I was awakened by the husband of one of the women in the pink house, saying they needed help now. I rushed over to find the baby presenting and on the next contraction the head came. Seeing that the cord was around the baby's neck, I slipped my finger in to move it, whereupon the cord turned to 'mush' between my fingers.

It seemed as if I was in slow motion, but others said that my hands flew. I was clamping what I could of the cord on the baby's end as well as the mother's. Then the baby slipped out on the next push. They were both fine.

Another time, I followed up on one of Francine's patients even though I wasn't supposed to do it. This mom had been laboring but couldn't quite push the head out. Feeling for the cord, I found it to be very tight, so I clamped it twice and Dad cut the cord. The baby about flew out after that.

Those were wonderful times, thanks to a great teacher who loved what she did. Sometimes it was hard not to allow whatever difficulties one mother had with another not to influence how we interacted with each other's children. To tend all the children while the other mother went to work or was away for a short time was not that difficult. Sometimes though, it was best to disengage emotionally. Just being sure that the children were fed and kept safe was the best you could do. Most of the time we were pretty well engaged with time outs and hugs that were dispensed fairly equally.

The other side of the coin was that Nelly had a problem with all of us, thinking that we didn't discipline our children properly. She was more than happy to step in at every opportunity, delivering what she saw fit, especially in our absence.

It was very difficult for me when my Daniel, who was so small at the time, would beg me not to send him to Nelly. Over the years, I have wrestled with this heart-breaking truth as he was in her care when he died years later. It was after the fact that I found out he was afraid of her because she would treat him unkindly. This is one of my deepest regrets. I, too, was afraid of her as she could stir up so much trouble. She would pretend to be so sweet but mean to my children in my absence.

Nelly was not the only one who left me with remorse when it came to Daniel. One time, the family was gathered in the front room, standing in a circle, holding hands for prayer. Daniel wanted to stand next to me, but for reasons known only to Nelly, she insisted he remain standing by her. He was only three years old at the time and, perhaps because he rarely spent time with his own mom, began to cry.

Everyone in the room stood riveted to the floor, incredulity on their faces, mouth open as they watched the scene play out. No one dared make a sound. The crying irritated Frank and because of Nelly's continued insistence that Daniel remain with her, Frank became furious. He forcefully picked up my boy, took him into the bathroom and shoved his little head under the cold-water faucet yelling at him to stop crying. I rushed after them, begging Frank to stop. Finally, he did and left the bathroom in disgust.

Holding my drenched little boy, I gathered my daughter, as well, and went to my room. This was the time, so many years ago, that hatred found a corner to hide away in my heart and mind toward that cruel man and Nelly as his well-suited wife.

It takes a long time to root out such strong emotion and I am not sure that I have been able to find forgiveness in this thing. I could not comprehend such shameful behavior on the part of grown adults. For many years to follow, I judged myself harshly for being so weak and spineless as to lack the courage to stand up for my son. After all, I was the only one responsible for his defense. It sickened me that the one person who should have been able to protect him, cowered before two bullies.

I have since learned that I did a normal thing in an abnormal situation as it was survival for us. Frank had power over me, the worst of which was the ability to take my children and place them with whichever mother he saw fit. Considering the influence Nelly had with him, I knew that it would undoubtedly be with her, an unbearable thought.

33

NOTHING SO COMPLICATED AS PERCEPTION

———◇◆◇———

PEOPLE, OR MY PERCEPTION of them: where lies the truth? It is fair to say that despite Frank's position on the council, he and his family were looked down on? We were in the basement of the group's social superstructure. Those who judged us had earned their place within the group or, so they felt, because their polygamist grandparents had been persecuted in the 1950s. They were the elite, at least that is how they portrayed themselves. There was most definitely a hierarchy.

Perhaps I can describe it in terms of old money versus new money. In some circles, old money is best because one has inherited it. Their family always had money, giving them a sense of privilege. New money, even if it is billions, must be earned. Someone had to get their hands dirty, so it is just not quite good enough. So, it was in the group, as newcomers were not quite as good as those whose families had been there for years.

Over time, I have reflected on this scenario. My feelings of never really being good enough—I cannot help smiling at the irony. The times when my daughter stood up for a child of one of those "elite" families when they were being made fun of at school. Kids would push them around and call them polygs. My family knew about the bad language those children used on the school bus but knew better than to use it at home. Their parents though they would never say such things but rumored that mine did. They probably did; I'm not that naive!

We lived down the hill from that family and there were times when some of their children would come to play at our home. They would all have a great time playing on the tramp, drinking Kool-Aid and eating popsicles, lying on the trampoline looking up through the branches of the big Chinese elm tree as the sun filtered down on them, jumping from its branches, bouncing with true abandon.

On one of those days, one of the visiting children took the liberty of telling me that I gave my children too many treats. Children usually don't come up with those things on their own, but they do repeat what their parents say. It seems that I was being criticized for sharing small treats. I felt foolish, as I had been trying so hard to be accepted by these people, to be one of them. Rejection is tough, especially when you're pretty sure you have made a fool of yourself.

Once in a while I wax philosophical about my place in the group. It was winter several years after the stinging realization that I would never be accepted by the people I once thought were so wonderful. I had moved to my home in Riverton, the back yard adjoining the playground of the elementary school. Looking out the window, watching children play, I noticed snow falling, those beautiful, large flakes, the kind that children will stick their tongue out to catch, then wait to feel them melt in their mouth, tilting their back while more snow lands on their face and their eyelashes. They close their eyes, extend their arms and twirl around until they fall down giggling while they make snow angels in the snow. Engulfed in the magic of the moment of such simple pleasure, nothing else exists. Uncomplicated clarity followed that moment. I could see those people from years ago who were so reluctant to accept me, with the uncomplicated clarity of a child encountering the snow.

Often polygamist children would be taunted at school or pushed off their bikes and similar cruel tricks. They learned to band together just as mine had. The other children had learned that if they picked on one of my children, they had just picked on all the polygamist children. Still, the memory stings, but it isn't until a day like this as the sun shines through and children are playing in the school yard that I stop and reconsider those feelings. While children build snow men and snow forts as the sound of their exuberant joy wafts into my home so reminiscent of the past, that deep reflection passes over me. With the benefit of a little experience, I feel my focus shift and with a breath of kindness can blow the chaff away.

34

THE LIBRARY

⸺◦•◦⸺

FRANK HELD THE BELIEF that there would be a complete economic, government and social breakdown of our nation sometime soon. That was thirty years ago. I honestly do not know what he imagined this would really look like. I do know that he was converted to the principal of poverty, and that he accomplished it extremely well. The idea of us living in primitive conditions at the Cedar Valley property was appealing to him as he thought that no one would know we were there. Perhaps he intended to join us at some future date. Or, was it an escape from providing for his family? Was it one of those out of sight, out of mind situations?

However he saw things, he began collecting books, mostly from thrift stores, on a multitude of subjects. They could be about anything from how to raise a guinea pig, to more scholarly and technical books. There were also children's and religious books, car repair manuals and periodicals. There seemed to be no end to the books he sought out. He would say that many major universities were built around some man's personal library and so it would be with his. Out of the ashes of whatever collapse our nation would experience would rise such an institution built around his library. Unlike Harvard or Princeton or any other well-known university, however, I could see that his books were fast becoming outdated and none were intrinsically or historically valuable. To facilitate this grand place of learning around his library, Frank established a private academy, legally registered with the state. I was an officer of that organization at one time.

On one occasion, while my children were small, I accompanied him on a book buying trip to a thrift store. I asked if I could look for shoes for some of our children, since many of them were growing out of their current shoes. He said that I could. I set out guessing sizes. How could I go wrong with so many feet to consider? Satisfied with my selection of about ten pairs, I met up with Frank. I had a big smile on my face, pleased that I could find so many pair in good condition. He appeared dismayed, surprised.

"What is this?" he asked.

"Shoes," I replied. "You said that I could look for some."

He just looked at me blankly and said that he didn't have money for shoes, only books.

I was shocked and looked at him in disbelief, feeling as though I had been slapped in the face. Why on earth would he say I could look for shoes if he had no intention of purchasing any? I had chosen shoes for my own children and for others in the family, as well. For a moment, I felt a flash of anger. My sister-wives and I were giving him everything: our emotional support, our time and our paychecks. We dug in the garbage to feed our family. We lived in rundown rental houses, while he hid out in his library. And he couldn't buy a few pairs of shoes at a thrift store? But soon after, I felt helpless, powerless and had no words to speak. He had defeated me so easily.

The books had become his top priority in life. His library was an obsession! The store in Midvale generated zero income and finally closed. Frank moved his books and remaining inventory to the yellow house. What had once been a lovely dining room and living room became lined with bookshelves floor to ceiling. They obscured the light that once filtered through tall windows. A third room eventually filled with books as well, leaving only the kitchen and bathroom. Slowly, the rooms upstairs were lined with shelves and books. Some of the rooms had double rows of shelves, all filled with books. Even the hallway upstairs was lined with shelves and what else? Books. Every possible nook or cranny had shelves, leaving only two bedrooms for the two mothers. A bathroom that they never could get the plumbing to work right in became a work area for the library.

I often wondered if Frank had heard of spontaneous combustion. With everything catalogued perfectly, he withdrew more and more, rarely leaving his sanctuary. Amidst the stacks of papers was a meticulously built-to-scale model for "united living quarters." There were floor plans drafted out in detail, only to be rolled up and put in a corner, never to see the light of day. Nothing Frank conceived of would ever come to fruition.

There were so many factors contributing to the collapse of Frank's elaborate plans. The Order was disintegrating. No one wanted to develop the Cedar Valley property. There were no pawns left to use and abuse. In an attempt to garner sympathy and rally support, Frank pleaded in regard to the property, "Is this only going to be known as Johnson's folly?"

But this was just another attempt to manipulate those in the room. As transparent as it was, I couldn't help but pity someone who had placed himself so far above everyone and everything in the real world. His lofty dreams destroyed, he was now broken and reduced to rubble. Pride is a terrible thing and by the end of his life, Frank had lost everything of true value. He was no longer respected by his peers, most of his family was gone, including wives and children, and he was only left with his books. I think that Frank never felt responsible in any way for the fact that so many had left, even the Order members who had fallen away. He never looked to himself for answers and therefore never reached out to those he once ruled over.

I suspect he thought of himself as being patient, waiting for us to overcome our rebellion and come back to him. But it was a passive patience, not requiring him to do any work. Some of the children, for one reason or another, had contact with him as adults. Others visited him when he was close to death. I saw him just before he died, and he had not changed a bit. The most I could charitably manage to do was to send him back to God with my peace.

The culmination of Frank's unyielding opinions, the need to have complete control along with wanting to be known for something monumental, built on the backs of others, forced him to forfeit so much of what life has to offer. What a high price he paid for his grand ideas of nothing. In his will, he left the library to the leaders of the group, for which they have shown very little interest.

35

PECKING ORDER

———◦•◦———

Without any doubt, there is a pecking order among sister wives. Women can be very territorial and will defend their numerical place. That is first wife, second etc. This seems to give them a sense of security and for some, superiority. It is not uncommon for first wives to tighten their grip on their husbands. Perhaps she feels threatened. Perhaps, he feels guilty for loving and taking another wife or maybe he feels more loyalty toward the first wife. In any case, she can keep her husband on a very tight leash. This woman defends her role fiercely. Traditionally, strangely enough, the first wife is sort of the second in command in the family.

Unfortunately, many first wives take this concept to an extreme. Setting herself up as the "Queen Bee." All wives are supposed to be equal. Different personalities, different qualities and abilities. This type of first wife sees herself as being closer to the husband than any of the other wives, more spiritual and more intelligent. Though she was not the first wife, Nelly aspired to this fantasy role. This necessitated her crushing Helen on every turn, pushing her out of the way to take her "place." If Frank asked Nelly to buy a can of shoe polish, she made it sound as if the fate of the world depended on her and her alone. I think it irritated her that the rest of us didn't care.

Somewhere between Big Love (I think the writers must have had some inside information) and *Sister Wives*, there is always some drama going on in a real-life polygamous family. One wife may feel that she can pull rank because she is the child of a council member—as Nelly was. Another wife may be insecure, another thinking she is being picked on, while another checks out emotionally and doesn't pull her weight. It never ends.

Some couples would have been married for half a lifetime before taking the first plural wife, creating a learning curve that they never learn to navigate successfully. Some young couples had only been married a year or two before anxiously awaiting another wife, the anxiety higher on the wife, of course. Some families, like ours, would be steadily increasing in the number of wives, showcasing the new additions. Doing so made theirs and our challenges more visible. I always felt like we were living in a fish bowl.

Ideally, wives should have absolute equality, but the sad truth is that one wife will try to rule the roost. It may sound harsh, but if you listen carefully, you will hear it said of one woman or another that, "She is the queen bee of that family." This means that she pretty much runs the family as she chooses. In the husband's absence, she rules, cementing her position and power in the family. Whether blatant or subtle, the pecking order remains.

Loyalty to one wife at the expense of the rest can and does prove devastating to plural families. I personally knew a family which was quite large at one time, with four or five wives. June and Sam had moved from California to be near the group and had several children by the time the second wife (Melanie) came along. June had no sense of boundaries, which is an essential skill to be learned as soon as possible for a polygamous wife. She would call Sam at Melanie's apartment about one of her children or nothing in particular and he would just up and leave with no explanation to Melanie. Someone must have asked him if he knew what he was doing. He said that he would go to June any time he wanted, making no excuse about it. He was an ex-cop and was very confrontational. Eventually, all of Sam's wives left him, leaving only June at the time of his death. When I think about this stuff, how one wife will be completely supported financially, or one has her husband's affection over others, the sticky road of having a favorite makes me sad. It would be better not to go into plural marriage at all as there is a high price to pay for that type of behavior.

My second marriage was also to a polygamist man, one who had a similar personality to Sam's and enjoyed conflict. The outcome was no better. My sister wife, Sally, in my second marriage, "enjoyed" a long life of ill health. Even her children gave her a hard time about it. She was as tough as nails but could appear frail and vulnerable. Evidently it paid off, garnering her the attention she craved. Many more times than once, our husband would hop out of bed at midnight or later to go to her because she was not feeling well, and he would not return. Maybe that doesn't say much for me. I respected her ability to manipulate the people around her.

I have seen other polygamous wives get a lot of mileage out of their health, or lack of it! Where was their self-respect? There is little enough dignity for a plural wife without having to fight for it like that. When I tried to talk about it openly, I was told that I was jealous. Even if that were true, it never seems to occur to the husband to find out why.

Then there is the funny side of things. For example, when new people came around the group, they always wanted to hear the first wife's story, of how she accepted the idea that her husband would become polygamous with a second wife. Maybe they thought they would hear some horror story or an angelic visitation. But they only ever wanted that story. As the fourth wife, I would occasionally find myself thinking, "What about the rest of us; we have a story too!"

Some families worked hand in glove, usually after gaining some experience, and that was really admirable. A story one of my sister wives told me was about her father's family. There were five mothers and their children living in a very large home, potentially disastrous. But she remembered it as a wonderful time, children running in the big yard and playing together.

As an adult, she looked back and could see that it was no easy feat, the mothers working around each other's personalities. They took a weekly rotation cooking for the family, a monumental task. Some of the wives would move the spices to where they liked them as they cooked. Then the next mother would move them back. It was a small thing, but I respected their ability to take it in their stride. This is not an easy way of life!

36

WHERE TO HIDE

———◆———

IN THE GROUP, THERE was always some type of impending doom hanging over our heads: an earthquake along the Wasatch Front, an epidemic of some kind, or something that would cause chaos and mob mentality and make you want to leave town. One of the least likely of these threats was that parts of the California coast line would break off into the ocean, causing the Salt Lake Valley to be flooded with sea water as it was when Lake Bonneville was here.

These fears accelerated about twenty-five years ago, prompting the establishment of several communities as places of refuge by members of the group in outlying areas. For many years, we expected to receive a phone call in the night to quietly leave our homes with the understanding that we would never return to them. I knew that Frank didn't prepare for anything. If I wanted there to be a plan,

I would have to manage it on my own. So, when I was living in the red house with small children, I took a shopping cart from a grocery store down the street. I had something that could loosely be called a twenty-four-hour pack, but not so well-equipped. My plan was to throw a couple of pillows in the bottom of the cart, then pile the kids in with everything else on the bottom rack and start walking. (I have since returned the cart.)

In this time, I was adrift in a sea of speculation, "woe be unto you" and quasi apocalyptic prophecy that poured over the pulpit with alarming regularity. No one ever prophesied happy things in the future. Instead, it was the constant negative, nebulous churning of nothing hopeful that kept my stomach in knots.

Some of my closest friends had a retreat in one of the communities in the west desert. One day they asked where I would go if we had to leave our home immediately. I'm not sure why, but this question hit me hard. I would have liked to go with them, but there would be no room. By that time, most of my children were grown and starting families of their own. I had beautiful grandchildren to whom I would give my last breath. But I was still caught in the fear of the future.

One morning, while looking out of my kitchen window as the first rays of light spread over the tops of the mountains, as clear as the warming sunlight itself, my answer came. I would not go secretly into the night to save myself. I knew that I couldn't just run away, not from my children and grandchildren. We would stay together as we always had. Fear had changed to trust.

37

BADGES OF HONOR

⸻◦•◦⸻

I THOUGHT THAT BADGES OF honor would be a great heading because that's exactly what it is—just a badge. These men are admired by and receive praise from their peers for certain things. To say this will sound strange is an understatement but is real nonetheless. The first badge of honor is simply the number of wives a man has. There are increments of number that are important to them, as the number of wives a man has is supposed to reflect his worthiness and overall goodness. I do not know the true significance of the numbers. A man with one wife looks to increase the number to three, "filling a quorum," they say. Next, he should acquire two more wives to become five wives, another "quorum filled," and so on, the sky's the limit. Mr. Jacobson, a one-time leader of the group made a startling comparison. Saying that a man with two wives is twice the man that a man with one wife is. Followed by, a man with eight wives is eight times the man a man with one wife is.

Adding fuel to the fire is the rivalry between the wives in the families as there is a pretentiousness that comes with being in a family with a lot of wives. In a sense, it is a win-win situation when it comes to prestige for husbands and wives because they all look good to the rest of the group. But, at what cost? It can backfire as things at home can only be more difficult. How much or how little do you want to see of your husband? When you just don't care how often your husband is home, the more wives the better.

When a man was courting a new prospect, the family would try to appear as nonchalant as possible, but it didn't take long to catch on from the inside. Yet the group was very big on secrecy, and it took me years to figure out exactly who was married to whom. This was intentional, since fear had passed from parents and grandparents who had experienced the raids in Short Creek. If marriages were kept secret, the government couldn't arrest anyone.

Superficially, the women in polygamy couldn't be happier, much like a duck swimming in a pond. The duck floats effortlessly on the surface, but paddles its feet like crazy under the water. I know, I have lived such a contradiction. It was refreshing, occasionally, to see young couples enjoying the happy, all be it brief, time of just being in love.

Another badge for the men is how many children each had. The final count in our family was forty-two. A lot of self-worth and outside admiration seems to be wrapped up in how many children women can produce. Large numbers were always impressive. One polygamous wife who had a lot of children, thirteen if I remember correctly, said that she had heard that children can make you or break you in life. She then added, "Frankly, I'm worried." I assumed she was afraid for her sanity. That was candid, as well as true.

The last is the most lamentable—even deplorable. Occasionally, a man would come into the group without his wife and children. Having been introduced to plural marriage, he was anxious to move forward toward his "badges," regardless of the damage done to that first union. Most "converts" come out of some church or other, so there is also a religious facet to the whole affair. Besides the shock and devastation of being told she is no longer enough for her husband, the wife will also have to sever her previous religious ties.

Almost without exception, a rift is created between both extended families, if she agrees to go into polygamy with her husband. Her parents blame her husband and the children are torn between them. It is a high price to pay either way. If she doesn't come, it's called "losing a wife." The first time I heard it, I thought that she had died.

This solitary male appears, bereft of wife and children. Sadness seems to sit beside him, but not for long. Admirers flock to him, lavishing praise and admiration on him for his brave stand and the sacrifice he has made. He is told that it is better to lose one wife so that he may gain more who are willing to live the "law." This is because the first wife would only hold him back, stopping his eternal spiritual progression. He is told that the increase in wives is what the parable of the servants and the ten talents in the bible is about. He reaches celebrity status with nothing much to show for it.

"Losing a wife" happens within plural marriage as well. I know one couple who were raised in polygamy. While they were dating, she told him that she didn't want to live that way. He looked into her eyes and promised her that he would never look for another wife.

Shortly after they were married, things began to change. Their home quickly became his parents' home and she was treated like one of the children. His parents began to put pressure on him to take another wife. Adding to his distress was the fact that his best friend had two wives, as did several of his friends that he had grown up with. In the end, he never did stand up for his wife, allowing his family to treat her with disrespect. He was too caught up in the assessment of others that he was a failure by comparison. It just doesn't look good to be a monogamist surrounded by polygamists. He was considered weak and a disappointment by his parents, whose own marriages were falling apart.

Apparently, crippled with the need for his parent's approval more than his wife's confidence, their marriage spiraled downward. After the birth of their first child, he began putting pressure on her to agree to his courting a young woman who had asked about him. After the birth of their second child, the very foundation of their marriage began to crumble. Reason gave way to argument, lies and deceit filled the air until he finally declared his intention to take another wife.

He knew he had to create an honorable way out for

himself, so the fights accelerated. One night he came home yelling in her face, "Are you ever going to live the principle?"

Broken by the tirade of words she was hearing, she shouted back, "No, not if it's going to be like this, I won't."

He had the response he wanted to hear and without another word, he turned on his heels and walked out the door. Shattered dreams filled the silence of their once happy home.

She felt he had lied to her from the beginning, but now she was the one being shunned and gossiped about. He basked in the light of congratulations from his parents and others who told him that he had shown great courage. He feigned sadness and sorrow at the loss of his wife. He would say things like, "I would give anything to get my wife back." He could have tried but did not. He quickly turned his attention to a young girl in another township and moved in with her parents. He was now sure to have a plurality of wives. All he had to do was discard one wife for a full hand!

What a catastrophic price he paid to live polygamy. The lies became easier, the deceit more frequent until it cost him his integrity. One has to wonder if a person like this, who has cast off his wife, ever thinks about how he has shattered the life of his wife, let alone his children. To bully and finally turn his back on someone he once promised to love and cherish? I wonder how it feels to crush the fragile flower that he once claimed to love more than life itself.

38

THE BEGINNING OF THE END

FTER A LIFETIME OF being pushed, I had begun to push back. I had been married twenty-one years by now. My children were in public school, were immunized and had birth certificates, as well as social security numbers. My youngest was seven and the oldest eighteen. I was fortunate to find records from Dr. Allred's widow, the one who worked in the clinic where he was murdered and obtained affidavits of birth from people who were present at my children's births.

At this point, Nelly had left Frank, abandoning her children and placing them in foster care. The number of children she had overwhelmed her and she had never wanted the responsibility of raising them. She was conflicted from the very beginning. I wondered if she had met someone who cared about her and treated her well.

Helen was weaker than Nelly and that seemed to give Nelly some power she herself did not have at some time. Paula and I were not so easy, but I feared her ability to convince Frank of her version of the truth. Nelly always had some drama going on. One time she had Frank convinced she had cancer–she is still alive. I think she wanted Frank to herself and tried hard to do that while keeping up appearances of a loyal and obedient wife. Paula and I were working and keeping our paychecks. Frank was losing his grip on me. However, he still had a stranglehold on Helen.

Because of the deplorable conditions Helen was living in, her uncle, who was the head of the group, placed her in a home owned by the group. He was paying the rent and utilities. Frank was furious, as he felt that the uncle was intruding into Frank's affairs, interfering with his family. "Crossing family lines," it was called. Never mind that Helen was broken emotionally and physically and continually shoved in some corner to be provided for by some other man at his family's expense.

While living in that home with some of her children, Helen was able to get work at a medical supply company, providing her with her first real sense of autonomy and dignity. She had always been in poor health. Having given birth to eleven children in almost as many years, her strength was depleted. She was easily overwhelmed by the number of children in her care and seemed to have given up.

In this vulnerable condition, Frank was putting pressure on her to quit her job and move into the yellow house, which was literally becoming wall to wall books. There was really no room for more people. The only space would have been in the unfinished basement. That house was like a morgue. It was cold and silent; each person lived in their pigeon hole, waiting to be readily accessed as needed, while Frank lived in his office.

Over about a six-month period, perhaps longer, Helen's children were attending public school. The children didn't mind her, would be late for school, not attend to their hygiene, often sleeping in their clothes and not doing homework. They didn't take lunches or have school lunch as Helen didn't know how to apply for assistance. In short, the children appeared neglected. I am not saying these things to reflect poorly on Helen; she was beaten emotionally as well as mentally and had given up trying to get the children to do what she asked. This is only to show why, eventually, social services became involved. It probably began with concerned teachers and accelerated from there.

Frank would not go to Helen's home to see her as husband and father, standing on his version of moral high ground. Instead, she was expected to gather up the children and make her way across town by bus, to the yellow house to see him. This would cause one of the wives to give up her bed for the evening. The other wife would end up sleeping on a couch and the children on the floor.

Without warning or conversation on one of these visits, Frank informed Helen that her son, Jack, would be living at the yellow house and attend the group's private school. Helen didn't like the idea. It wasn't that the private school was a problem, but she had a good idea of how the sterile environment would be. His every move would be regimented, and he would be coached to become another

Frank.

Weeks passed, and Helen was becoming desperate for Jack's sake. She said that the social worker was insisting she have Jack returned into her care. It was with this explanation that she begged me for my help. I was nervous, not wishing to make things worse between Helen and Frank, but the pleading in her eyes overcame my fears. The fact that I was in the process of getting a divorce from Frank, which he was aware of and that I would not have to answer to him probably gave me courage.

Picking Jack up from the private school, I was silently praying that all would go smoothly. As we drove up the hill toward the main road, I could see that some utility work was being done. Part of my prayer was that I would be shown or told in some way whether I should proceed, preferably not by the engine falling out of my car. Some less drastic way would be appreciated.

Just as we approached the men at the gate, a man stepped out, smiled and waved me through. I took Jack to his mother. After returning home, I called Grace, who had charge over Jack in the yellow house, to tell her what I had done and not to worry. I can only imagine the fallout and was glad not to be the one to tell Frank.

A few years after that, Helen died, from of all things, emphysema. She hadn't smoked a day in her life. Perhaps the smoke from the fire at the pink house began the disease. Almost from the time I knew her, she seemed to be looking for the day when she would be released from this life and from its demeaning, oppressive weight and ever-present sense of never being good enough or smart enough, as well as being abused and neglected by her husband. There was a late-night call from one of the children informing me of their mother's death and asking if I could meet them at the hospital where Paula joined us. It broke my heart to see her frail body lying there with the intubation tube still in place.

One of the children said, "Aunt Karen, please take that thing out of her."

"I can't," I replied. "The hospital has procedure it has to follow!"

Paula and I comforted these grown children as best we could. Once again, they became our children and we wept together.

Amidst the sadness, I couldn't help thinking of Helen slipping out of her body. She was finally free of her limitation. I imagine her singing with her beautiful voice and dancing with joy as her hair moved with her. I could imagine her embracing her parents, grandparents and siblings who were waiting for her, as well as Daniel. She died on her birthday—Happy Birthday, Helen. She was free at last to be who she really was.

39

ENOUGH IS ENOUGH

———◦•◦———

THERE COMES A TIME when you know enough is enough and it is time to leave. For many years before my experience with plural marriage, no women were given a "release," as it is called. Frank would say that it was to save them. Women who wanted to leave polygamy don't really know what they want. That when they passed to the other side, they would see what a glorious husband and family they really had. They would be grateful to him that they had not been given a release. Some women simply went away and were considered damned but never released. If they asked the council for help, they were sent home to overcome their weaknesses and pray for their husband. More recently however, a few women had been given releases. After more than twenty years, it was my turn.

I was already keeping my paycheck. My children and I were not attending Frank's Sunday school or family meetings, but he would still visit me about once every two weeks. I knew that he would arrive shortly after ten in the evening, then leave right after six am prayers. We were like strangers sleeping in the same bed, barely speaking. I never knew which day he would come. I would become anxious as the time drew near. Then dread would set in. I knew what I had to do.

Finally, guilt ridden though calm, I drove to the yellow house where Frank spent all his time to tell him I wanted a release. I think he was shocked but could not have been surprised. Grace and Betty hovered nearby, as if their united front would persuade me otherwise. I told him that I was going to speak with the leader of the group and Frank asked if he could come with me.

Together, we drove to Arthur's home, where I expressed my desire. I said that I could not remain in a marriage where I did not love or respect my husband. Shaking his head, Arthur asked Frank if he could not see there were problems. Couldn't he see this coming? Frank replied that he had seen some problems but that he was being patient. This was so typical of Frank's philosophy, intent on seeing himself as infallible and superior, he would not lower himself to approach a wife or child and try to work things out.

Even though his family was leaving in droves—two other wives had left already—he silently waited for them to realize they were wrong and contritely return to him. He remained true to his view and never reached out to his children.

I told Frank that I would not prevent him from seeing his children, but I wouldn't make it happen either. He made no attempt to see them or to talk on the phone. There was no birthday greeting or Christmas card. Evidently, they were "released" also.

Driving home after the conversation with Arthur, I was crying bitterly, feeling that I was worthless and the only thing I could do was cause sadness. I was surprised at how much this hurt me. I don't think Frank was hurt but his pride must have been. I was not elated or excited about what my future might bring, only grieving the end of something I had put so much of myself into. Arthur wanted me to be separated but not released. That would look better for Frank, but how could I live that way? I had to be persistent and finally the release was official.

I still believed in plural marriage and after about eighteen months, I began to think about remarrying. There was one man I thought was wonderful. He was also on the council, and that was probably the biggest factor, but can you imagine—he was not going to come near me with a ten-foot pole! It would have been awkward because Frank was still on the council, too. In retrospect, I had consistently shot myself in the foot with this man in expressing that I couldn't subject myself to a husband who felt it his responsibility to whip me into shape. The problem is, that is exactly how he would have been if he had been unfortunate enough to be saddled with me. So, I guess it turned out to be a good thing.

Some of my friends were pushing me to get married again but I was going to take my time. You don't just date in polygamy; it's more complicated than that. Young men and women must go through their fathers and gain permission to date or what is better known as "getting to know each other." For the not so young, you still don't just date, because there is likely a wife or two at home.

So, if a man wants to date you he is supposed to first have the consent of his wife or wives. He then must obtain permission from the head of the group to ask you out. If my father were in the group, the man would have to obtain his consent to get to know me, too! I did go out with a nice man, following the rules, of course, but it didn't work out.

I should mention that when you date in the plural world, it must be with the utmost propriety as there are other lives involved. I was a grown woman but still, protocol had to be followed. At this point my plural friends were getting frustrated with me saying that I would become too independent and would not want to get married again. It's not good to be single for so long, and wasn't anyone good enough for me.

About a year later, I ran into a couple I had known previously. I had met Jake and Sally years ago on one of our trips to southern Utah to visit a small group of people associated with the group. I remember thinking what a nice couple they were, and it even crossed my mind *What if I had met them before Frank and Helen*? I knew Jake to be a good man, and he was mannerly. Not only that, he had a job. A man without a job was a deal breaker for me at this point. I wasn't so sure about Sally. They had been married for fifty years by this time.

To show how ridiculous this culture is, you could say

that I came with good references. The mother of my dearest friend of fifteen years assured Jake that I wouldn't give him any trouble. So he could be however he wanted and I would be sweet and lovely.

Jake and I dated for a while before the agreement was made between the three of us to marry. Jake worked out of town and had to return to work that Monday. So we were married Saturday morning and spent the rest of the weekend at Park City, which is a local resort. The plan was that Jake would fly back to Salt Lake every weekend. That meant that I would be with Jake every other weekend.

I think we each, all three of us had unrealistic expectations. Sally told her daughter that she didn't see how her life would change much at all. Jake probably didn't either. I was thinking that I might have to remind him that he had another wife to consider because some men tend to neglect their other wives. It did not turn out that way! Jake was thinking more along the lines of life as usual and that he was only responsible for Sally. I was buying a home and would continue to do so as I wanted to have something to fall back on financially. I also had children at home, which can be the kiss of death for some second marriages. I guess they didn't help much, anyway, since my children were often disrespectful and really didn't know how to have a dad around. It presented a constant struggle.

Jake also believed that these were the "last days" and favored a scripture from Isaiah which says that seven women will cling to one man. The scripture says: *I will eat of my own bread and make my own cloth, only let me be called by thy name.* This scripture was interpreted to mean that the husband had no other responsibility other than giving a woman his name. I had apparently fallen into that category.

My children could see that I was still struggling financially, and that Jake was rarely around. Some would say that this was none of their business, but I was their mom and they were being protective of me. This caused the older kids to lose respect for him. He was much more comfortable in his own home than mine, and spent most of his time there, coming to my home only when I was there, and he would be staying the night. This type of struggle made it easy for Jake and Sally to go on trips together once he was retired, without saying a word to me. I would hear about it much after the fact. It was difficult knowing that Sally knew everything that passed between Jake and myself whereas I was in the dark. They were still living monogamy. I did work a lot of hours and had a couple of children at home but it felt that I was invisible.

These two issues, unrealistic expectations and children, would become the catalyst for the downfall of our marriage. The sense of just being an appendage became overwhelming and the glitter of living the "law" had fallen off for each of us. At one point, I had broached the issue of him only providing for Sally. I think in frustration, Jake said to give him my utility bills and he would pay them.

I knew that Sally wrote the cheques, so I didn't want to do that. Then he asked how much they cost so I told him that it was about a hundred dollars. I was equally frustrated. From that time on, he would leave a hundred-dollar bill or the equivalent on my night stand once a month. I felt like a hundred dollar a month hooker. But every time,

I thanked him for helping me. We were happier apart than together.

For many months, I had a medical problem that had become offensive to him and an embarrassment to me. It was my suggestion that he stay at Sally's until I was better. Drifting further apart, he never came back. Eventually, I boxed up what was left of his clothing at my place and put it in the garage. When he came to pick up his stuff, that's where he found it. He never even came in the house.

I don't believe in placing blame. There is plenty to go around. Our experiences make us who we are, and I am appreciative of them all.

40

WHAT MADE ME LEAVE

━━━◦◆◦━━━

T HE SUM TOTAL OF my life experience to this point had brought me to my knees, but not in a cleansing way, as some things can. Mentally and emotionally, I had reached the bottom. I couldn't find the wherewithal to push up again, even enough to break through the water to get a breath of fresh air.

I had now been married polygamously and "released" twice, which does not bode well for a woman. The first failed marriage I have written about at length, the second I think was due to a combination of inexperience coupled with unrealistic expectations and the inability to communicate for both of us. What relationship there was had deteriorated into a technicality that neither of us was interested in prolonging. He'd always lived with his first wife. I couldn't continue living in limbo, just being an appendage. So, I took the initiative to end it, which was simple enough.

But my problems with polygamy had become more than about individual men. There were actions by some of the leaders that were just not right and stories not adding up. I was seeing things in a different light; women were property while children were always the casualties.

Arthur had died, and Harold was called to fill that spot in the council. I had spoken with Harold several times, trying to find a solution to my quandary. I had allowed myself to be completely vulnerable. I poured out my deepest feelings, spiritually and emotionally. I asked for a favor that is not usually utilized or readily given. It was my last hope of being able to continue in plural marriage. I asked to be sealed (married) to the deceased husband of my two closest friends, as we had so much in common spiritually and it would have been wonderful to have them as sister wives.

Harold said, "Absolutely not. There are plenty of men who need to live the law." Surprisingly, my dilemma had become all about the number of men seeking a good word to assist them in obtaining another wife. It felt like a cheap game.

But from Harold, there was no kindness, no gentle word, no relief, and no hope. I knew that he didn't hold me with much esteem. He was the one I wanted to marry after I was released from Frank, when I thought better of him.

Now I felt sick and betrayed. My feet worked, but my head didn't. How could this be? It really was true that unless I was willing to be a submissive, obedient woman, there was no place for me in the group anymore.

I knew the men out there in the group and the way they treated their wives. I had no attraction to anyone. However, I was expected to choose someone, marry him and consummate the marriage. I was supposed to jump back into the fire, live the life I had already lived. My head was swimming.

I could not do it! I knew that God didn't expect that of me. As I left Harold's office, I asked if I was still under the protection of the "priesthood" in a spiritual aspect.

In what seemed a disgusted tone to me, he replied, "Oh yes, anything you need. Let me know."

So, just as I stumbled into this way of life, I stumbled out. It was unbelievable! Invisible and without value this is what my sixty-five years had become.

41

THE ROAD BACK

I SAT ON THE BACK deck of my home in the still, early morning hours, watching as the neighbor's cat returns from a night of hunting. Birds swoop from our big Canadian Maple tree flying tantalizingly close to him. There is a family of quail in the concealing lower branches of the climbing rose bush on the back fence. It pleases me to watch them race about in line, parents attentive to chicks. The Hummingbird tree, at least I think that's what it's called, has tufts of bright pink flowers on it. Finally, I think it will survive.

Survive! That is what I seem to do best. The culmination of the past thirty-five years has brought me to an abyss. I feel a sadness, a grief of sorts that I have failed the test. Am I just not good enough? Did I not give all that I had within me? Why could I not make my marriages work? After all, it was supposed to be my one most important task. The dark clouds of disillusion and disappointment have engulfed me for so long that I have begun to question everything about myself. I feel no peace. You know that time of night when you wake up and all the ghosts of your worry come out? You go over and over your thoughts until they seem to become redundant, but they are real, and you would give anything just for some hope? Then you know how desperately I needed that hope.

From around my late teens, I have lived my life from a spiritual or religious frame of reference. I had no doubt that Jesus was my only source of true strength and guidance. I also knew that I would need the friendship of fellow believers, so I decided to simply go back to my original LDS church! That may seem rather simplistic, but I didn't know how I would be received. I made no attempt to hide my past and in time had revealed all. If I was to become a new person, deceit would have no place in my ongoing life.

The ensuing weeks were filled with a mixture of feelings and emotion. Even knowing that I was on the right path, whispers from the past, like icy fingers, played with my reasoning. Nonetheless I found myself surrounded by kind and generous people, lifting me and loving me.

As I settled into my new stage of life, I found myself actually happy! I had confided in a friend at work and her support was comforting and invaluable. There was a perpetual smile on my face, sometimes accompanied by a giggle, which was a little embarrassing if someone noticed.

It took time to reveal the huge changes that were taking

place to my co-workers. One day while sitting in the lunch room, the Sister Wives show became a topic for discussion. One nurse spoke up and said she would like it because the new wife could be the housecleaning wife. Another said it would be okay, as the new wife could do the grocery shopping and it went downhill from there.

At that time, no one knew about my life, so I sat quietly thinking that they had no idea of what it was like. My old acquaintances would be inclined to say that of course I would be happy. I was no longer living the "law." They would say that those who leave are deceived or weak and so can only be happy if they are allowed to live the way other weak people do, without polygamy.

Others would say that at least I went back to church instead of going off into the world and being lost. It was not at all surprising, as I had said the same thing myself of a woman who had left her husband. Life swings on small hinges! It was intended as a kind of consolation prize, second best, if you know what I mean.

Well, my consolation prize turned out to be the jackpot! One night as I was falling asleep, I realized that I felt peace, deep comforting peace. No longer was my pillow wet with tears of sadness but with tears of gratitude and hope.

Most of my life, I have had the feeling of being driven, in a way. I have had an intense sense of purpose, which was to find my way back to my heavenly home, to never take my eye off that goal. I still desire that, but now my vision was expanding, reaching out to others to share my joy.

42

BREAKING OUT OF PRISON

———◦•◦———

Not all was smooth sailing. It seemed that at times, I needed something to heal my soul. In most ways, I had turned so far inward that I felt numb. My children saw me grieving, though it was different than it had been in the past. For so many years, I had wanted them to be with me in polygamy. Now it seemed that life was in ruins. Contradictions ran wildly through my mind. What if they had stayed with me? They would be in the same place I was escaping. I felt inadequate, a failure, and at the same time cheated because I could not go back and get my son Daniel from his grave.

It wasn't until I took a long, hard look at myself that I saw I had built a wall of self-righteous grief, isolating myself and completing my miserable emptiness. That is when I turned to my Savior, who taught that the only way out of my well-crafted prison was to forgive.

It's not easy, breaking out of prison. It is especially difficult when you have built it yourself and are ever so familiar with each emotion and the reasoning behind every action that has cemented every brick in place.

For so many years, I was only aware of the task before me, routinely going about each day like a human robot, rarely connecting with anyone, let alone my own family. Slowly and deliberately, I learned to be 'present' when my family was around me, chipping away at the damaging habits of the past. I learned to allow people to love me and to reciprocate. I was having real conversations with my children and taking time to play with my grandchildren.

I think I have become a better grandmother than mother. A few years ago, two of my grandsons were into dinosaurs and we would hunt for fossils. Anything we found would qualify as a dinosaur "tooth" or "egg."

One day, I bought some huge bones from the butcher, cleaned them well and then buried them in a patch of dirt in the back yard. Next time they came, I told them that I was pretty sure there were dinosaur bones in the back yard. They dug for a long time, not stopping until they found their prizes.

I became aware of how rewarding it was to call each one, from time to time, telling them to have a wonderful day at school. They probably wondered what on earth I was thinking, but it was fun!

I think that little by little, we are healing each other with these simple acts. I have no doubt that love is the sustaining force of life, nourishing and strengthening, as nothing else can. As I look back over the years, I don't think that even one of Frank's children has escaped their childhood unscathed. From another mother's point of view, I could be wrong. It could be only my observation that all have struggled to some degree or another. Some children were wounded very deeply, such as those who were molested. The children who were abandoned, then placed in foster care and were not able to keep in touch with their siblings could not have come out of it unscathed. Additionally, those whose mothers didn't know how to cope with so many children, the children whose mothers worked many hours out of the home and then tried to play catch up had to have been impacted, at least to some degree.

This all created enormous cracks in the foundation of the family, which many fell through. Nonetheless, they have pulled through. Some of the children are now in some branch of the medical profession. Others have become skilled in one trade or another. Most all have a marketable skill at this point. Others are a strength to their spouse in their careers. Many now have happy homes of their own, while some are stalled in that arena.

Some were diverted for a while in ways that were not compatible with a successful life but have made their way through just the same. There is one thread that runs through each life. That seems to be perseverance or the ability to get up and try again no matter the opposition. It pleases me to see the way some of the children still feel free to reach out to the remaining mothers for guidance or reassurance. We are able to shelter them as we once did a long time ago.

Watching my daughter become a mother herself has

been a wonderful thing. Seeing her bonding in a way that only motherhood can bring has been pure delight. Witnessing her ability to spoil those little ones is truly impressive. Seeing my children become loving and attentive parents, aunts and uncles, as well as, moving forward with life is a testament to the resiliency of the human spirit There is something that comes with us into this life. It is seeing who we really are and that from whatever ashes there may be, we can truly rise to heights whose limit is only that of our own faith and love.

43

WHAT WAS IT LIKE?

EVER SINCE I CAME "out of the closet" so to speak, I have been asked many questions about my life. They would range from intimate to general things, such as what an average day was like. To set things straight, there was no kinky stuff!

To answer some of those other questions: Every day started with the family being awakened for 6 a.m. prayers, for which there were no exceptions or excuses. If I was lucky, my baby would stay asleep. If the stars were smiling, my toddler would hardly rouse and then my other children would pile back into bed for an hour or so.

Even if a mother had been up through the night with a sick child, she was still expected to get up and bring the child with her. This would make prayer into an exercise of our husband's will. Family prayers were set for 6 A.M., noon and 8 P.M., like clockwork. These times were set so that no matter where we were, the family would be praying at the same time. It wasn't a bad idea really, but the strict adherence to the schedule took away from what it could have been.

Most of the time, it was chaos, lots of children and mothers working out of the home or absent. This put a lot of stress on the mothers at home. There was not enough room or money for our needs. This was all punctuated with hard work. Sometimes, it was like living in a pressure cooker: the heat was always on and someone was ready to blow their stack.

We tried to keep to a schedule for meal preparation and household chores and leaned heavily on the older children for help caring for the little ones. It was a big job to be the mother at home with so many little ones. Each mother was responsible for getting her own children ready for the day whether it be home or school, and we took turns preparing school lunches. Wow talk about an assembly line! Everything was done on a big scale. Even when I lived with only my children, I would overcook. It's hard to go from around twenty-five to five.

Getting greens (dumpster diving) was always a big day. All the mothers and older girls were expected to help clean and put them away. Laundry was also an adventure as we often shared a washer and dryer with another family, especially at the pink house and at Butterfield Canyon. We did our own. I became an expert at timing the wash cycle, so I could get another load in before someone else showed up.

I suppose my life was a lot like other working moms.

I just had the feeling of living at the speed of sound and blindfolded because we were not included in decision making.

I have been asked if I have any regrets. Well, yes. Most of all, it is that I had to leave my children so much. It wasn't just going to work. It was the extra things, like greens and working at the book store, which all added up to a lot of time away from home. Sometimes, I would try to slip out, so the little ones wouldn't see me leave and cry.

I also trusted Frank. Wrongly, as it turned out. It never occurred to me that he would take advantage of that trust. I wanted to live plural marriage to the best of my ability and with integrity, which didn't always benefit me.

Finally, I regret that I deprived my mom of the happiness of being around her grandchildren. For a long time, she didn't know where we lived and even when she did, we were only permitted a few visits. Being a grandmother now, it breaks my heart to see what she missed.

What about greens? Was I embarrassed? The first I heard of greens, as we called it, was the story Nelly told of having one of her boys with her when picking some bread up from a store. She had told the employee that she had pigs and that was what the bread was for.

As they left the store, the boy said something like, "Do we have pigs, Mom?"

I would go with her at first and it would make me smile as we wheeled out shopping carts of food. Pretty soon, I became the major greens person. I figured out a route I would follow depending on when the stores discarded the food and when the garbage trucks came. At first, I was embarrassed if I was in a bin and an employee came out. But after a while, I had no shame, as we all depended on my success.

What about jealousy; what about it? It never was a concern of who Frank slept with and when. I didn't care much about that, actually. I think that must sound strange, but I wasn't connected to Frank in that way. My main insecurity was that I wanted everyone to know that I made sacrifices for the family that others didn't. I really wished we could trade places and there were times I was ticked off and resented remarks about me being the one to work at the bookstore. At least, that was my perception of things. We were walking a tight rope of emotions while juggling our responsibilities.

Occasionally, the subject of "the library" comes to light. It was something I thought I had put behind me as I had no control over it, not now or in the past. Except for driving past the yellow house almost every day for years and just shaking my head at that mausoleum and what it stood for, I didn't give it much thought.

(Come to think of it, mausoleum is a fair description as the home was probably quite stately in its time and for a moment, held the remains of one narcissistic man's sole focus in his life. The avenue by which, he believed, untold numbers would come to him for instruction, directly or indirectly, a type of immortality.)

Some things can only be appreciated by way of contrast. When part of the family moved into the yellow house more than twenty-five years ago, it was home to three mothers and nine children. There was a large dining room with an adjoining living room, Frank's office and his growing library which swallowed up two bedrooms on the main floor. Sunlight would stream through large windows until the mothers were told to cover them so that no one could see inside.

Notwithstanding the friction that comes with living together, the house was full of life. The thundering of children who were confined to the house, so as not to be noticed, was gradually curtailed as it was too noisy for Frank in his office. The front staircase inside was closed off to prevent traffic in that part of the house. That left only the back stairway open to traffic, which could have been disastrous in case of a fire.

In the end, Betty was the only wife living there as Grace had died. Bookshelves took over and silence filled the house. Slowly, the home seemed to die. It became choked with books. Only pathways to navigate from one part of the house to another remained of the once vibrant home.

After Frank's death, Betty was the last wife standing; with the house itself came all those books and papers. It was a truly daunting bequeathing in my mind. Driven by curiosity, as well as sympathy, but mostly curiosity, I made myself available to help. But in the end, Betty had to move out of the yellow house with short notice because the family of the man who owned it wanted to sell it. She had been paying rent that had remained the same amount for thirty years. I asked Betty if I could see the old house again. As I was taken through the house, Betty unlocked each door, then locked it behind us, each door proof of the secrecy that was Frank's way of life. It began to feel like the prison it had become, at least for Grace, as she was restricted to only small parts of the house and eventually died there. I have called it a morgue, and even without Frank there, it still felt cold, dark and lifeless. Betty had to find a place for all of Frank's books because the council was not interested in taking over the library, even though he had willed it to them.

One evening, on the way home from work, I noticed that there were lights on in the house, so I stopped to see what was happening. I could hardly believe my eyes. There were probably fifteen pallets of boxed and wrapped books with as many waiting to be boxed up, to be shipped to some repository. Not until that time did it really sink in, just how many books there were. My mouth worked to get words out but could not find one to express my astonishment. Not only that, but in one large room, there were bookcases seven shelves high, built and reinforced with two by fours. If there were an earthquake, the house would probably have fallen, but those shelves would be left standing!

As it turns out, the library is supposed to be digitized at some archive address, so anyone can access them. This is probably a better option than the dump, which was my first thought. I can't help wondering, if the economy or nation collapses as Frank believed it would, will anyone be able to access his precious books anyway? Thinking about that, I have to confess, made me smile. Looking at the sheer number of books, then converting them and the lumber into money, there must have been many thousands of dollars represented. Who can understand a man who would put his books before the care and wellbeing of his children? I don't, but that is what all those books amounted to.

Revisiting the past only gives it power and my anger, which I have experienced plenty of. It only harms me. So, leaving judgment to a higher power, I can only put it down and walk away.

44

MONEY, MONEY, AND MORE MONEY

———◦◆◦———

OVER THE YEARS, THE fundamentalist group we were part of has been awash with one great new business "opportunity" after another. Each one was bigger, better, and more certain to bring success than the previous one. Start-up money and the right connections were always minor obstacles. Some men seemed to be a lightning rod for these schemes, pursuing them relentlessly instead of earning a living. There were a few who were more ambitious than others, who did not allow the odd shady deal to stand in their way. The husband of one of my dearest friends was sent to jail because of one of these deals. I always felt that he was a scapegoat while others got off, who should also have been locked up.

I don't think many people knew what was happening when the "Virginia Hill" money was being moved around and laundered. Anyone with access to the internet can follow the gist of Virginia Hill vs. AUB. It involved a Las Vegas resident who was supposed to be investing in a land purchase. At first, it was supposed to be in Nevada but was later changed to a ranch in Utah. There was a lot of cloak and dagger going on that eventually landed a banana box full of cash on the desk of a prominent group leader.

There was hearsay that a lot of money was channeled through group-connected businesses; donations in cash going in, and a check written going out. No one deals in large amounts of cash in business. It generally involves checks, money orders or bank drafts. For all the denial, what part of a box full of cash does not bring the thought of money laundering to mind?

But in the end, only one of those named in the suit served any jail time. The larger fish skillfully slipped through loopholes. Though the group leaders cried persecution and proclaimed their innocence, the court still ordered close to a million dollars to be repaid. I thought they would have to sell some property. But, oh no, the faithful members were told they were expected to ante up to the tune of a thousand dollars per adult and more.

People sold vehicles. Others took out loans. Some others ended up using what savings they may have had, leaving good people in financial difficulty.

In another instance, a leader embezzled a large but undisclosed amount of money from the group with virtually no repercussions. Little or no recompense for serious offences propagates the idea that these people are above the law, as they seriously believe. Others follow suit. What a mess. Funny how stinky fish can be!

NOT CONNECTED WITH THE Hill case, but involving one of the men named in it, who will have to remain nameless lest I be sued as it is not part of public record, did something truly despicable. His first wife evidently was unable to have children and shortly after the second wife gave birth, he took the child and disappeared with him. I remember seeing the mom from time to time, thin and worn with despair, her eyes lifeless and almost hollow. The word on the street was that he had gone to Australia along with his first wife. But that was only rumor. During the Virginia Hill case, documents proved he did go to New Zealand.

I had known the couple when they first came into the group and spent a lot of time associated with Frank's Order. I thought they were sincere and good people. I guess I was wrong!

Some of the men in the Order messed around with drugs, trying to reach a higher plain. He was one of them.

45

WE WERE NOT THE ONLY ONES ...

━━━◁►◉◄▷━━━

Lincoln and Rita

L INCOLN AND RITA JOINED the group in the late
1970's. Predictably, they were not warmly welcomed
by old-time members because that is just how it was.
Becoming affiliated with Frank didn't help to endear them
to pretty much anyone but those in his Order. Over the
years, Lincoln married two other women, both of whom
eventually left him.

Rita was not able to have children. She became the
working mom. As far as I knew, she was a good mother to
the other wives' children. It did seem that Lincoln had a
very military approach toward his family, but then I was
only seeing from the outside in. I think it would be reasonable to say that he quickly learned the tools of the trade of

a man dealing with several wives. Control to these men is as a hammer and nail is to a carpenter.

I lost track of them until recently when I stopped by their home, looking for an address.

Lincoln knew that I had left Frank, but not that I had left the group as a whole. He welcomed me with a "*step into my parlor, said the spider to the fly look.*" This made me very uncomfortable as he proceeded to invite me to join them for a discussion group which was held on Sunday evenings.

I felt a ripple of panic as I swallowed hard. I was sensing the ooze of charisma so commonly used when a man is about to the spew forth the sticky, entangling, virtues of the so-called "higher law." Much like a venus fly trap, the woman is enticed by such a performance. By then, it is too late.

I was quick to let Lincoln know that I was no longer in the group and very happy as I was. I met his new wife of perhaps two years, who seemed very nice. I couldn't help wondering how she could be attracted to this man, let alone with the evident poor circumstances he was in.

Wait a minute, I did exactly the same thing! I'll bet that people were shaking their heads at me, just as I was in dismay at her choice. One becomes engulfed, then cut off from the outside, unable to see beyond the enclosing wall and unable to make comparisons.

Now to the real issue, I had encountered Rita a time or two, of late, at a local store and was surprised to see that she was not the bright, dynamic person I remembered. The life had gone out of her; her eyes were dull and saddened.

She seemed defeated, lost and unsure of herself. I later found that Lincoln and the second wife Linda, had moved to another state to start a business, leaving Rita to fend for herself and maintain their run-down property. Lincoln would visit her in town from time to time but without notice. It kept her on a very short leash.

When I first called on Rita, she seemed nervous and couldn't understand why I would contact her after so many years. On subsequent visits, she was defensive of Lincoln, especially when I suggested that she had been abandoned. Professing happiness and devotion to the principles she had been converted to, she felt that this separation was the price she was to pay to be faithful. It was a holy sacrifice of sorts. She said that she was lucky to have Lincoln.

My head almost exploded when she said that! It is so typical that the polygamous husband does whatever he wants, when he wants and with whom he wants. The wife or wives just must deal with it! Rita did not know that Lincoln very smugly bragged to a neighbor that he had her right where he wanted her and that she was not going anywhere. I only know about this because this neighbor is a friend of mine and is concerned about Rita. I couldn't bring myself to tell her about it.

At my most recent visit, she seemed to be more open as we discussed different subjects, although she seemed still to be so empty, an outer shell, her true self having been devoured by her husband's will and apparent criticizing. She expressed the need to overcome weaknesses, such as jumping to conclusions, or misjudging and not having sufficient information to form an opinion.

I suggested that this was a lifelong quest and that we should all be trying to become a better person. She said that she thought she talked too much, as evidenced by our conversation. Lincoln had made a point of saying that Rita talks too much. She is so lonely and starving for validation and acceptance. It's palpable. She told me that he had told her that if he wanted her opinion or input, he would ask for it. Just the way to crush a barely beating heart in one sentence.

I asked her why they didn't sell the property and all move together. Rita said that she had to overcome her weaknesses, that she had so much to work on. The idea of overcoming weaknesses seemed to consume her.

Pressing her, I asked if moving together was dependent upon her apparent state of worthiness. Her entire demeanor changed. Her body pulling in as tightly as it could. Her head hung down as if the weight of the universe was pressing in on every direction and she said, "Yes."

Have you seen how crumpled a gas can becomes when the air is sucked out of it and the air pressure crushes it? That is what she looked like. My heart ached for her. I wanted to take her home, to protect her and help her to heal.

Unfortunately, she is the only one who can do that; she must fight for her life. Rita, as with almost all plural wives, has been stripped of all sense of self, having morphed into her husband's ideal of who and what she must be to be a good wife. These women surrender their hearts to their husbands', their minds to their husbands' teachings, believing that he is their ultimate head and he alone knows what is best for them.

As a post script of this story, Rita has moved out of state with her husband and sister wife. She was able to get a transfer with the company she has been working for and now she supports the other two financially. Lincoln and Linda live out of town on a farm of some sort. Rita is now much less independent and more easily monitored by Lincoln.

46

ANDREA'S STORY

LIFE SEEMS TO SWING on very small hinges. Or, is it just karma? You decide. Andrea was the daughter of a council member and his second wife. It is safe to say that she and all of her siblings were raised with the expectation that they would follow in their parent's footsteps. Her parents had joined with another council member in purchasing two lots of land in a suburb where they shared costs in building and maintaining the homes. The families interacted freely. The children played together, and the adults took on the role of aunts and uncles.

One of the closest things to arranged marriages that I have seen is when a father tells a man that he has a daughter for him—to marry, that is. The father would strongly persuade his daughter toward his older friend. The pressure is usually pretty intense, much like in long-ago history where kingdoms would be united by marriage. No one thinks anything of it if a young woman is married off to an older man. There is usually a lot of attention given to the girl who is swept off her feet as much as that is possible. Her dad would be very pleased with her obedience.

So it was for Andrea. Soon after high school, she was married. A couple of children later, Andrea realized that the income she was making was not going to go far. She was on her own financially and her husband spent most of his time at other homes. Her husband offered no solution so she enrolled in a computer science program and was able to be financed through a grant.

Once she had graduated, she went to work for a local computer company. Several times, she was sent out of town for training and later to problem solve for companies her employer serviced. Sometimes, it would be with a co-worker who happened to be male. She began to make better wages, deciding to move to a nicer home. This was the point when her husband suddenly became jealous and accusatory and began looking for inconsistencies in their conversation which did not exist. He confronted her often and she would have to defend herself in front of his peers.

It is impossible to describe how their marriage deteriorated. However, she eventually asked for a release. Very few women before this time asked for one and none were given. It was a courageous act for Andrea. She was subjected to several rounds of the most graphic questioning in front of the council. The foulest accusations of immoral conduct were made as they demanded she speak the truth, which she did. Throughout that disgraceful display, she maintained her innocence. Her reputation was sullied, while gossips fanned the flames of stories that grew with the telling.

Now here is the irony: Her husband, who had accused her so harshly, was accused of child molestation spanning many years. Some of his own children and grandchildren had come forward, saying that he had threatened them if they ever dared to say anything against him. But I suppose their pain outweighed their fear of him.

This man would deny the charges repeatedly until some of the mothers of those children came forward. He called them liars, but he was finally dropped from the council. Outraged, he left, taking some wives and children with him. Much like my own husband, only some children were molested by their dad so that others were free to continue to believe his innocence. Now both men have passed, leaving a trail of damaged lives behind them, never confessing their deeds.

47

LAST BUT NOT LEAST

──◦•◦──

Marion's trap

URING THE BOOK STORE years, two couples who were friends for some years came into the group, each with some children. As you may surmise, the more converted the men became, the less happy their wives were. They attended Frank's cottage meetings and became committed to him and the blossoming Order. These families lived in the same home, which became crowded very quickly. Each man took another wife. Earl took two within a year. The men became very controlling, dictating their wives' every move.

Marion, Earl's wife was becoming disenchanted with the whole affair. Earl became restrictive regarding Marion's interaction with her family, who lived out of state. As with most, her love dwindled as her husband's grip on her increased. A mistake on her part was that she told Earl she was leaving and taking their children with her. From that moment, she was not permitted to leave the house with all her children at the same time.

She came to me to see if I could help her, but there was nothing I could do. The children were held hostage while she had become a prisoner. She was very carefully watched by the adults in the house who were reporting her every word and action to her husband. Had she left with some of her children, the rest would have vanished with their father, never to be found. How could she sacrifice those left behind?

The last I heard, they had all moved to another state, creating a commune of some sorts, cutting ties with us. Earl was very much into the idea of his family being his possession, much like a pot or a pan.

48

CONCLUSION

———◦•◦———

BECAUSE THIS IS A true story, I have changed the names to protect the innocent and infamous. It has not been my intent to vilify Frank or anyone else, though I may have done a good job of it. It's just the way things and people were, as I saw it in my story and on my journey. I have been harsh regarding male attitudes toward their women, but I think they deserve it, as truth is truth.

All these events are to the best of my recollection, along with prompts from my journal. There is also some input and reference points from some friends, some of whom are still in the group. If you were to ask a sister wife about one story or another, she would probably say that it happened a little differently. But, by and large, she would agree with it. We see things according to our experience and bias, so there is bound to be some diversity.

ACKNOWLEDGMENTS

M Y SINCERE APPRECIATION TO Heather Moore of Precision Editing who gave me hope when my manuscript was barely recognizable. Thank you to Crystal Liechty and Mette Harrison, two most excellent editors and delightful ladies, who encouraged and prodded me to do more and to do better. Thank you to Karen Christofferson of Bookwise publishing for her invaluable advice. Thank you so much to Dayna Linton of Day Agency, who guided my every step through the unfamiliar process of layout, design and publishing. My thanks to my son, Ben, who helped me to bring thoughts to paper and putting up with the highs and lows of this experience.

Finally, thank you to my friend Donna Hill, who assured me that this story must be told.

ABOUT THE AUTHOR

KAREN MILLER WAS BORN and raised in Sydney, Australia. While living in Canada, traveled to London and Paris, finally locating in the United States. She has worked at the University of Utah hospital as a unit co-coordinator for twenty years. She is the mother of six children, grandma to six and great-grandma to three, all the source of much joy.